I0485460

Credit Repair

How To Repair Credit And Remove ALL Negative Items From Your Credit Report Forever

By

Richard Stanton

3rd Edition

Table of Contents

Introduction

I want to thank you and congratulate you for choosing the book, *"Credit Repair: How to Repair Credit and Remove ALL Negative Items from Your Credit Report Forever"*.

This book contains proven steps and strategies on how to repair credit and remove ALL negative items from your credit report forever.

We all want to have a nice credit rating because we understand that this makes access to credit easy and affordable; that's why we will do whatever it takes to ensure that we don't do anything that might threaten that rating. What happens when your efforts don't bear the needed result in boosting your credit rating? Credit repair might be the best solution for you. In any case, why should you pay more when you shouldn't? This book will walk you through the process of repairing your credit to ensure all negative items are removed from your credit report forever.

Nowadays, credit is extremely important given that most people use it almost every day like it is a part of their daily survival. These include credit cards, house payments, and car payments among others. Regrettably, many people fail to consider their credit rating until they are involve into trouble dealing with it.

When you have a bad credit rating, it can affect not only your ability to obtain a loan. It may also result in problems in terms of securing any type of credit. For instance, you may encounter problems when renting a property, paying deposits on your phone lines as well as other utilities, or getting a store financing. As such, it is necessary to pay attention to your credit rating.

On the other hand, if you have a bad credit rating, there are several possible ways that you can do to carry out a credit repair. The first crucial step is getting your credit report. You should know that all information regarding your credit is reported by your bank and other financial institutions that you are involved in to credit bureaus. In turn, the credit bureaus are the ones holding the key to start implementing the credit repair.

More often than not, people pay less attention in obtaining their credit reports unless they are already in a situation for credit repair. It is important that you get a copy of your credit report regardless of what your credit rating reflects.

In general, there are no fees or charges when getting a copy of your credit report. In most instances, you only need to request for it in writing coupled with a valid identification card, which you can photocopy.

In the event that you are turned down for a loan or credit card, you should ensure that the company provides you the information as to which credit bureau reported you as being on a bad credit. Then, you should already request for a credit report from the credit bureau.

If you are attempting to carry out a credit repair, you need to take time in looking into your credit report. There are cases wherein credit reports have inaccuracies or discrepancies. For instance, your credit information may have been confused with another individual's file whom you have the same name with. There are also cases wherein there are erroneous data on your credit file. There are many cases in which people are surprised with reports of missing payments by mistake.

Should you find any inaccuracies or discrepancies in your credit report, you can carry out a credit repair by requesting, usually in writing, that the concerned credit bureau conduct an investigation on the disputed items. In your request, you may include a supporting documentation, if available, or simply state your dispute and request for an investigation.

By doing this, you will be able to have the inaccuracy removed from your file if the credit bureau is unable to verify the information of your dispute. In addition, if the credit bureau fails to respond to you within 30 days, the disputed item should be removed. If your bad credit is proven to be a result of a mistake, all you need to do is to go to the concerned credit bureau and ask for credit repair. When you are requesting that your credit be repaired, keep in mind that most credit bureaus would make the process appear more taxing than it is, specifically with regard to taking most of your time. Some credit bureaus would give an impression that they are not interested in responding to requests for credit reports.

This is just the first step that you should take when attempting for a credit repair. More efficient ways on repairing your credit will be discussed in this book as well as how you can improve or avoid having a bad credit rating.

Thanks again for purchasing this book, I hope you enjoy it!

Chapter 1

What Is Credit: Why Should We Bother Keeping It High?

I wish to thank you again for choosing this book and hope you have a good time reading it. In this first chapter of the book, we will look at the meaning of credit and why it is vital for you to keep the score high.

Credit simply refers to the ability to borrow. We all need money to cater for various expenditures in life. However, just like any other economic resource, it is never enough, which means we are limited to what we can do since almost everything nowadays needs money. In this day and age where consumer price rise is quite apparent, it is getting tougher and tougher for the average person to afford a lifestyle. Right from consumer products to services, everything is now extremely expensive and the person needs to arrange for bagful of money to lead a normal life. But it is not possible for him or her to arrange for this money through their monthly income alone and have to rely on some external sources of credit. These sources of credit can be banks, credit card companies and other creditors, who will readily give you credit, if you fall under the desired category.

For instance, without additional or external financing, individuals and corporations cannot expand or grow financially. It is important that they have some money at their disposal in order to cater to all their monthly/ yearly financial needs. Borrowing is one of the most reliable sources of financing there is available but of course, it comes at a cost.

Nothing in this world will be only about benefits and there will be several good things that come with a price. That is, this cost of borrowing is closely tied to the credit score, which determines how high or low your interest will be; different people will pay differently based on their credit score. It will depend on whether they are good candidates to repay a loan on time and whether they have the capacity to pay at all.

Although most companies will have strategies in place to help them repair their score, the same cannot be said about individuals. An individual will have to fend for himself and there won't be others who will rush in to help him and control the damage. Therefore, you need to look after your credit score yourself and make sure that it is always high.

In essence, the higher your credit score is, the less interest you will pay for credit, which means that borrowing becomes favorable for you. The opposite is also true; the lower your credit score, the more interest you pay, which means the costlier it will be to borrow. This might seem unfair but that is how the system works. The credit company will not take a risk on someone that they think are not worth giving money to. To be safe, they decide to charge these people much more than they would normal people i.e. those with a good credit score.

To put it into perspective, your credit score is closely linked to your mortgage, car insurance, life and health insurance, car repayments, utilities and cell phones just to mention a few of the things closely related to your credit score. So anything that deals with your daily upkeep will be related directly to your credit score and in order to avail these, you will have to pay attention to it and maintain as high a score as possible. Interestingly, employers now check your credit score before hiring. So it is important that you have a good score in order to be ready to start your financial journey.

As you can see, having a messed up credit score will probably make your life as far as finances and access to various products and services a living hell. You will not have a chance to lead a normal life and in fact, when your credit score is in bad shape, you probably need a miracle to live in your dream house or drive your dream car just to mention some of the things you could probably miss.

This is not an exaggeration and is meant to tell you how important it is for you to build a good score and maintain it for as long as possible. You will need a roof over your head and your own vehicle to ferry around and without these it will be very difficult for you to live normally. Not just you but your family members will also have to compromise if you don't have a good credit score to help you avail these luxuries. Therefore, you cannot think of it as being a light topic and must focus on getting your credit score back on the right track. So, if you have any hope of attaining different financial goals, keeping a good credit score has to be one of your top priorities.

Chapter 2

Understanding Credit Repair

In the previous chapter, we looked at the meaning of credit and the importance of maintaining a high score. Now, we will shift focus to what it takes to repair your credit and why repairing it is a vital aspect for improving your credit worthiness.

We all know that your credit score is one of the greatest determinants of the kind of lifestyle you are likely to lead; that's why we do everything in our power to ensure that we keep it favorable because that in itself determines how much it would cost us to borrow.

As was mentioned earlier, you need to borrow money in order to lead a normal life and borrow money to afford the various basic necessities. We also looked at how it is important that you consider how high or low your score must be in order for you to avail credit. Bear in mind that the credit reporting agencies have to report everything pertaining to your credit in order to enable future borrowers to ascertain what rate of interest to charge.

It is their duty to do so as they will have to remain in the good books of both the creditor and the one borrowing. They will report something in its entirety regardless of whether it is the truth or there is something wrong with it. We all know that you will probably pay more as your credit score goes lower and lower. You will be charged a bigger rate of interest as it will help the credit company remain safe. So, this means that the lenders will be making more money for lending money to you when you have a poor credit score compared to someone who has an excellent credit score.

Even as we work so hard to make ends meet so that we can maintain a high credit score, it isn't uncommon to discover that your credit score has slipped lower due to some inaccurate entries on your credit report, which means that the cost of borrowing goes higher. Irrespective of the time you discover that erroneous items are on your credit report, you can start doing something immediately to fix the situation.

Remember that springing into action as soon as possible is vital and you need to remain alert. This process of doing something is what is referred to as credit repair. So, what happens when you are trying to repair your credit? Although the process could be lengthy, the process entails disputing the specific incorrect, erroneous and any unverifiable entries in order to compel the credit bureaus to remove those entries from your credit report. This will help you clean up the mess and fix a bad score. Although it is not possible for you to do this yourself, you need to put in all efforts to have it fixed for you.

It is your right to have correct information reported on your credit report. Why would anybody want to have bad credit owing to wrong and erroneous entries? Is it fair for the individual to have a bad score without any mistakes of his own? Of course not! And for this, you need to take the right steps to fix your bad credit rating. Actually, the Fair Credit Reporting Act (1971) clearly puts it that you have the right to dispute entries in your credit report. You also have a right to get a free copy of your credit report every year, which means that you can check what information has been included in your credit report within that period.

Although the law doesn't clearly tell you to dispute incorrect, erroneous and unverifiable entries, the fact that you have the free copy of your credit report means that you can identify anything that you are uncomfortable with and file a dispute. This is only meant to help you with your credit score and make you more reliable to creditors. You cannot sit back and wait for your credit to fix itself and as soon as you spot errors, you must get to having them fixed.

This coupled with the fact that the FTC clearly states that you can improve your credit score by yourself (http://www.consumer.ftc. gov/articles/0058-credit-repair-how-help-yourself) means that all hope is not lost as far as fixing your credit is concerned. Even if the law doesn't tell you to file a dispute if you find any erroneous, inaccurate and unverifiable entries in your credit report, it provides an enabling environment for you to dispute. So you can start to approach the authorities to help you have the errors removed or your score fixed through some means.

For instance, the fact that numerous laws have been put in place to enable credit providers to deal with identify theft and fraud alerts means that you really have some legal backing to ensure that accurate information is published on your credit report. It is your right to have the right score and no one can stop you from having the correct figures mentioned.

The Fair Credit Reporting Act clearly states that it is the duty of every creditor to validate the accuracy or validity of any data contained in a credit report once a credit consumer disputes that information. This means that once you file a dispute on erroneous, inaccurate or unverifiable entries, the creditor will have to validate it or have it removed from the report. This will automatically help you fix your credit score.

Many people wonder if this validation will show badly but it will not. If some erroneous entries were made without your knowledge then you have all the right to challenge it and have it fixed. It will not show badly on your part as you only did something that was necessary for you to rectify a mistake.

I know that sounds fairly straight forward! However, keep in mind that neither the credit reporting agencies nor the credit providers have any interest in having your credit score looking exceptionally good. So they will not jump to help you or themselves take the initiative to fix your problem.

The truth is they make more money when your credit score is bad so why would they want you to have a great credit score when they stand to lose revenues in the process? Everybody thinks for themselves in this world and your creditor will do the same. As long as your account will show bad credit, he or she will be glad to serve you and pull as much money from you as possible. But if they have a chance to help you fix your bad score then they will be least bothered as it will affect their business.

All credit reporting agencies are privately owned multibillion-dollar corporations whose number one priority is profits; they care less about you having a good FICO score. This means that they will definitely want to sabotage your efforts geared towards disputing entries in the credit report; that's why I compiled this book to help you get through the entire dispute process easily and allow you a chance to take the right steps in fixing your bad credit. But do not panic. Although they will put in efforts to block yours, they might not always succeed. You are in the right and they are in the wrong, so it will be easier for you to win the battle. You need to take the right steps and you will get a chance to fix your bad credit score.

To start with, you have to understand how the credit system works, how you can beat the OCR and e-OSCAR computer systems that the credit reporting agencies use, how to use the Fair Credit Reporting Act to your benefit and how to use other effective credit repair strategies to fix your credit. Many times, just fixing your mistakes will do the trick and your credit score will improve instantly. Add to it getting rid of any erroneous entries and you will have a chance to have an extremely high credit score. In any case, you are the only one who has interests in keeping your credit score high so you have to know how to do everything on your own!

So, you now understand why you have to keep your credit score high and some basics on whether it is possible to repair your credit. You must remain determined to have your credit fixed no matter what the circumstances. However, it is one thing to know that the law is on your side as far as disputing inaccurate, unverifiable and erroneous entries is concerned and another to actually get those entries removed from your credit report. Just by noticing that there is a mistake will not help it in getting solved.

You need to take steps to correct it. It will be quite a process and you will have to gear all your efforts towards cleaning your credit score. It can sound like a daunting task but you need to do it in order to avail a good score. To enable you a clear understanding, let me explain how this is so by showing you how the credit system works. The following chapter will carry a detailed explanation for how the credit system works and what you can do to fix bad and erroneous entries from your credit report.

Chapter 3

How The Credit System Works

By now, we have looked at the meaning of credit and the importance of maintaining a high credit score. We also looked at what credit repair is all about and now, we look at how the credit system works in order for you to understand the process of credit repair better.

In a nutshell, the entire credit system constitutes the credit bureaus, the creditors and you. Creditors are the companies you access credit from while the credit bureaus collect credit data from past and current creditors and compile it into reports, which are modeled in form of credit profiles for each credit consumer, after which they sell these reports to the creditors so that they can make various decisions.

The creditors use the data they obtain from credit bureaus to determine how much they will charge you for borrowing and the amount of penalties they should charge you for defaulting. Whenever a creditor needs credit profiles of people that have a certain credit score, they buy that information from the credit bureaus. This helps them to target their products and services since they will then send emails to those in that list enticing them to buy or use their products and services. It is believed that most of these companies go after those that have a low score. This will allow them to have a chance at making a greater profit and pulling out as much money as possible from these people's pockets.

And so, at this point, I should perhaps highlight that sub-prime credit data is the best selling product for credit reporting agencies. If you are in this group of credit consumers, you will get the most enticing offers and email solicitations to apply for credit cards. The reason is simple; as was mentioned, when your credit score isn't so good, the creditors will definitely charge more for advancing you credit, which means that they make more money. In financial terms, creditors address their exposure to credit risk through charging more for credit. This means that if you have a very good credit score, the lenders will not be interested in doing business with you since you won't bring them any substantial money either. You will have the capacity to pay the right amount on time and this will cause them to not have a substantial amount of profit. They will not be satisfied with what they receive and will want more out of their customers. They might not directly refuse you credit but will not be particularly interested in giving you money. They will be waiting for someone with bad credit to walk in. Actually, when you have poor credit, you might be paying up to three times what you would pay were you to have a perfect credit score.

So the companies will expressly go after those that have a bad score and will put in all possible efforts to trap them. As you can see, creditors will definitely be inclined to prey on those with sub-prime credit score for the simple reason that they will make more money from you; even if you were to default, they will have made money already! So there is a lot of planning that they will do just to fill up their pockets.

It should not surprise you that these companies work hand in hand. It takes efforts from both ends for their scheme to work and they will ensure that they are on the same page. They will come up with plans that will benefit both and cause each to make a large profit at the expense of the customer. Imagine trying to cheat millions of customers on a yearly basis, it is a herculean task and will require the doer to remain as prepared as possible to pull it off with ease. For this reason, they will join hands and make sure each one cuts into the profit.

Apart from these 2, there will be some third parties that will work in helping these credit companies. These can be outsourced companies or independent ones looking to hook up with the credit companies and trying to make money for themselves. These will have the exclusive job of looking for people that have not checked their records for some time and determined to get them on board. They will put in a lot of effort to catch these people's fancy and once they trap them, they will direct them to the credit company and get them to pay for their services.

To prove that your bad credit history records are a best seller for credit reporting agencies, do you know that they will even charge more to credit providers to access such information. That's right, they will pay up a little extra just to find those that have a bad credit and start bombarding them with emails that ask them to apply for credit at their place. This means that none of these parties has any specific interest to have the information in your credit report reported accurately.

Do you know that that only a small percentage of people actually file disputes for such items despite over 90 percent of credit reports having been found to have erroneous, unverifiable and inaccurate entries? Many will not wish to go through the pains of proving themselves right. This allows the companies to avail a long leash and they will not back away from exploiting these people. The companies have several field days owing to such ignorance on the part of the customers.

The credit companies will be determined to report your bad credit and this means that some of them will even let such entries to be included in your credit report for the simple reason that so few of us have the guts to challenge entries in the credit report even if they are incorrect, unverifiable and erroneous. They will know who exactly will not challenge it just by looking at your credit history. They will not have an interest in catering to those that might take up disputing. They will employ people to especially look for those customers that have a bad score and those that look most likely to remain mum about errors in their reports.

The 2 other players in the credit system (the creditors and the credit reporting agencies) are in it to make the most money from you directly or indirectly so counting on them to help you make things right should be out of the question. Actually, the more screwed up your credit score is, the more money there is to be made by the credit reporting agencies and the creditors. That is, the lower the score the better their prospects to charge you a bomb.

So, when you file a dispute, the creditors and the credit reporting agencies will only update the data not because they have any interest in your welfare but because they don't have an option given that they are under legal obligation to act in accordance with the law. They will not expressly pursue your cause and in fact, despite your efforts to fix your bad score they will try and remain ignorant of it and make things worse for you. They will go to any length just to make sure that you have no chance of fixing your score despite none of it being your fault.

This is the exact reason why there are hundreds, probably thousands, of people who despise credit card companies. They will not stop at anything and fall to the absolute lows just to make a few extra dollars. Many of these companies will have a bad reputation and yet find easy prey for themselves. They will know how exactly they can target the customers and get them to subscribe to their card. Once the person is trapped, they will not stop until they fulfill their desire to make as much money as possible. The poor customer will be trapped and will have to surrender to the demands of the vicious company.

Every day, there are hundreds of innocent customers who fall for this trick and do not put in efforts to check their credit reports. But it is important for every person to thoroughly go through their report and look for any erroneous and wrong entries that is causing them their low score.

Now that you understand that no one but yourself is on your side on matters pertaining the accuracy of the credit report, how do you know how your credit score affects your ability to borrow? It is apparent that you score is the most vital element in your report and something that needs to be looked into carefully. But what is this score and what are its parameters? How do you know that your score is good, average or bad?

Of course the report doesn't state that a certain amount is bad, so understanding what benchmarks the lenders are going to use in categorizing you as good (perfect), average (sub-prime) and bad will be very helpful so that you know what to expect when you see that number on your credit report.

To help you understand this better, the next chapter will be dedicated to credit scores and what each category means. You can relate your score to one of these categories and understand where you stand.

Chapter 4

Good Or Bad Is Your Credit Score?

In the previous chapter, we looked at how the credit system works and as promised, this chapter will help you interpret the credit scores.

In a nutshell, your credit score could range from anywhere between the low 300s to mid 800s. These are the general score ranges that are considered by credit bureaus and credit companies. It should be apparent from this that the 800 mark is the highest and the 300 is the lowest.

As you already know, having a poor credit score will determine how much it costs you to access credit. The lower that it gets the worse your interest rates and the more money that you spend, however, we looked at how companies will flock to target you and try and get as much money out of you as possible. These figures are set based on calculations that are done by the credit bureaus. Depending on your credit history, they will add up your debts and come up with a number that will help determine where you stand.

To help you understand the scores better, here is a breakdown of the credit score ranges and what each means. You might probably find that your credit score is pretty bad than you thought!

720 and above-Excellent
When you have this score, you get the best interest rates and repayment terms for all loans. This score can come in handy if you are hoping to make some major purchases. You will avail credit without any problems and at the lowest possible rates. But then, this score is extremely hard to establish. You will have to put in

a lot of effort to maintain this core and still, you will not come anywhere close to 800. The most you can wish is to come close to 720 and remain there for as long as possible.

680-719-Good

When you are in this category, you will get good rates and terms but not as good as those with excellent scores. With this score, you can get favorable mortgage terms. You might not face as much problem but will have to be ready to run around from company to company to have your credit approved. Again, this score is not very common. You need to put in extra efforts to get it over the 680 mark. If because of some erroneous charges you are not able to cross this limit then you must try your best to get it cleared as soon as possible.

620-679-Average

When you are in this category, you can get fair mortgage terms and have it easy when buying smaller ticket items, (of course with no better rate than good and excellent scores). Take care not to slip down to the level where mortgage is unaffordable. You must keep an eye on your credit report and if there are unnecessary entries then immediately take action to fall back in your previous range. There can be many in this range or just miss out on it owing to bad entries. This range is average and most people with an average income will remain here.

580-619-Poor

When you are at this level, you only get credit on lenders' terms. You will probably pay more to access credit so be ready to pay more. Also, you should remember that you cannot access auto financing if your score goes lower than this range so you should work towards building it. This is where a large majority lie. Their score will be bad mostly owing to wrong entries. If you lie here then you will have a tough time getting credit in your budget limits and will have to be ready to pay up a lot of money.

500-579-Bad

If your credit score is in this range, access to credit will be quite high. Actually, if you are looking for a 30-year mortgage, you could be looking at, at least 3% higher interest rates than how much you would pay if you had good credit. On the other hand, if you are looking for something short time like a 36-month auto loan, you might probably pay almost double the interest rate you would pay if you had good credit. So being here is probably the worst thing that can happen to your credit report. You cannot possibly be here and hope to get away with low interest rates. That is next to impossible.

Less than 500

If your credit score goes to this level, it is so bad that it might be almost impossible to get any type of financing. If you do, the interest rate will simply be unfathomable. You might have to spend 30 to 40 years trying to repay it. Your entire life will be dedicated towards repaying a loan and might only get free by the time you are 50.

I am sure several of you are in this last range. But don't panic as help is at hand. You might wonder if it is possible for you to fix your score if you are in this category and the answer is, yes! It is possible for you to improve your credit score and possibly enter the good range.

Understand that no one wants to have his or her credit score bad for the simple reason that access to credit will be too costly. It will be the worst type of score for any person to have regardless of their borrowing habits. That's why it is paramount to take action when you start seeing inaccurate and unjustifiable entries in your report. If you spot errors that are causing you to be in this range then you must spring into action at the earliest. To help you understand what's at stake here, let me explain to you what is at stake and why you should start following up on everything reported on your credit report otherwise you might end up paying more for credit than what you ought to; you don't have to learn the hard way.

To start with, I will explain some few facts about the credit reports just to put you on high alert on matters related to your credit.

➢ A large proportion of credit reports have erroneous, unverifiable and incorrect entries; to be precise, 93% of credit reports have been found to have incorrect entries that affected credit score negatively. So, do you know what that means? It means that you and I could be having entries in our credit reports that we know nothing about; actually, we might simply discover that our credit score is ruined when our loan application is turned down. You need to look for these entries after gaining a free copy of your credit report. Now, as you have seen above on what each range of credit score means, by the time you get to the point of being turned down for a loan, your credit score is pretty much bad! You might start falling in the below 500 range and it will simply mean doom. The tiny details you see on your credit score that you don't understand where they came from could be the ones ruining your credit score. What happens is that lenders will often make some minor changes when reporting data to the credit bureaus some of which taint the credit consumer's financial reputation.

For instance, a change in the date of last activity on your credit report should be something you should start worrying about; when you have something derogatory appearing in the recent activity items, your credit score will be tainted. This might be completely imaginary or a simple manipulation of your actual entry. You could even have noticed different creditors reporting the same debt multiple times in which case; your credit report will show that you are really sinking in debt even if this is not actually true. These might be some extra large values, which will only make your score appear bad. You might also have noted the same creditor reporting the same debt in your credit report under various account numbers; this has the same effect as having multiple creditors reporting on the same debt.

Obviously, creditors could defend themselves as not knowing that these mistakes existed. However, they really care less about that because the worse of your credit score is, the more they charge you for credit. As was said before, they will stoop to any low just to get you in a fix. They will not care about your side of the story and stick to what they think is their right. So you need to be alert all throughout and do what is right for you.

➢ The law requires that creditors can only keep information about your credit history for just 7 years. However, it isn't uncommon for lenders to keep this information for more than 10 years, which means such items will probably continue showing on your credit report year in year out, which in turn messes your credit score after which the lenders raise the interest rates you pay. They will not be accountable to anyone and will claim to have erased any information in regard to your credit scores. But they will keep using the date to bombard you with target specific mails and offers.

The answer to these inaccuracies in credit reports lies not in sitting around and expecting your creditors to have mercy on you because they won't. This is the problem that most people suffer from. They will think the creditor will empathize with them and help them reduce their bad credit. But they will, in fact, be interested in ruining your credit score further so that they have a chance to pull more money from you. So, the best idea is to instead, start with you doing something about bettering your score and not wasting any more time.

In any case, why do these corporations (lenders) want you to pay them for something you shouldn't pay? You must understand how these companies will try and trick you and remain alert. If at any time you find out you are being cheated owing to mistakes and errors in your credit report, you need to spring into action and deal with them at the earliest. But what must you do to repair your credit as soon as possible?

The credit repair process can be complicated and frustrating especially if you don't know what to do. You might get lost easily and not have a clear direction. Actually, trying to dispute on your own without first understanding how to go about it could probably ruin your chances of ever succeeding; that's why most people probably give up on their trial because they never did their research well. You might ruin something that can be fixed easily and worsen your credit score in the process. So it is better to exercise precaution and try and do all the right things.

Knowing you have the right to dispute and actually disputing successfully are two totally different things; I will teach you what to do throughout the process if you are to emerge successful in the dispute process. The key to getting derogatory items in your credit report deleted permanently is understanding and following the tested and tried credit repair process otherwise you might simply start going in circles where you get an item removed and later restored in the credit report within 60 days.

So it is vital for you to start doing the right things and move in the right direction to have your score fixed. To start with, you need to start going through every detail in your credit report if you are to know what entries are derogatory in the first place. This means doing a thorough perusal to find what is wrong with your credit report. There could be a lot of errors and you need to look at each and pin point at them. You can then easily have them rectified. But you can't do that if you don't have up to date reports. You need to have all the reports that will clearly show all your entries. But where should you go to get these updated results? Well, let's take a look at where and how to get them.

Chapter 5

Resolving Bad Credit Situation

Most people who are regarded as a bad credit risk is likely to be shut out by the same society, which flourishes on credit. You may find this such a huge contradiction. Being marked as having a bad credit may result in having deep internal wounds. This is because, naturally, you would not want your neighbors to find out about your bad credit. Worse, it would be a dishonor in your part if your entire community would found out and be the topic of their gossips.

In truth, however, you do not have to deal with this type of mentality even if you have a bad credit situation. This issue is only a result of exaggeration from federal authorities and financial institutions that almost 40% to 45% of the people are in a bad credit situation. Consequently, when you are considered as a bad credit risk, the doors that were previously open would most likely be closed, which is one of the downsides of bad credit. On the other hand, you need to understand that having a bad credit is not the end of the world. Bad credit only implies that future financial institutions will be careful when carrying out transactions with you. For instance, you may be obliged to pay earlier than you used to, which is to be expected. Besides, if you were in the shoes of these financial institutions, you would also do the same.

Fortunately, there are a number of enterprises and people who are adept in repairing a bad credit situation. Furthermore, there are books, e-books, videos, DVDs, and cds that can educate you about various credit situations.

If you are already in a situation of bad credit, it is best to use real money when purchasing instead of plastic, such as credit cards. This can help you spend less and you will be inclined to avoid even the most effective marketing strategies of companies. You need to get a hold of yourself by learning the techniques and tools on how you can cope with your bad credit situation. The key is to fight the situation in order to restore your good financial state as well as your dignity.

Credit Repair and Bad Debts

Bad debt is a term used for describing one's accumulated result of his/her previous financial misdoing. It leaves a black mark on one's social and professional life. The first step to get away from the stigma of bad debt is to have a complete makeover of your financial situation. You can do this by not repeating the financial mistakes you have committed earlier. In addition, you should do away with your negative financial habits.

There are various ways to correct your financial state, especially when it comes to credit. One, try clearing your debt in a shorter repayment period. This way, your loan amount would not be tagged for many years. In addition, you can prevent yourself from another bad credit through a shorter repayment period.

Two, go for loans with less interest rates. Your loan amount should have an interest rate that you can repay in a monthly basis.

Three, opt for mortgage loans that have lower interest rates and taken on collateral basis so that the creditor would be at a low risk. Unlike bad credit unsecured loans, secured loans are granted based on the property, home, or asset of the borrower.

Four, you can search online portals that offer various types of loan deals. If you have a number of options, you can select the most suitable loan deal for your needs and capability to pay.

Five, you can get a student loan, which not only improves your credit score, but also enhances your professional and/or education skills. Furthermore, when your skills are improved, you will get a better-paying job.

Finally, make sure to keep a regular repayment method so that you can avoid tension and worries. When you pay your dues on time, it can increase your credit rating.

There are bad debt loans that serve as a practical solution for every financial problem. These loans are common in the United States and United Kingdom. Bad debt loans can help you pay multiple loans with varied interest rates. These loans can consolidate your numerous outstanding debts into just a single loan from one specific creditor instead of having several lenders.

Through managing your finances efficiently, you will be able to turn a mistake in the past into something positive. When you apply bad debt loans properly, you will be able to recover from your poor credit standing. In addition, you can save yourself from going into a worse financial state.

Some Simple Tips on Resolving a Bad Credit Situation

Probably the worst situation that a credit card holder would be in is a bad credit situation. Apart from hindering one's current life, it can also affect the potential of applying for or securing a loan.

There are several factors that may lead to a bad credit situation. The most common of which is overspending. This is considered as the most considerable factor that result in a bad credit situation.

Another factor is the non-payment on time. More often than not, people, especially credit card holders neglect paying on time for their different purchases, which later affect their credit history.

Inevitable conditions such as unemployment, health problems, and financial setbacks also lead to having a bad credit situation. These are conditions wherein people are left with no choice but to spend without considering their credit scores.

Fortunately, there are various ways to improve your credit score through proper rules, which can help you resolve your situation on time. First, you can check for the consistency of your credit report. This will ensure that no wrong information and mistakes are included in your report. Should there be any inaccuracy, make sure to report it at once to the concerned credit bureau or creditor to carry out the necessary correction.

Second, it is best to keep a budget for your expenses. This involves discerning the items, which added considerably to your bad credit rating. It also involves saving money to repay debts and controlling yourself on overspending.

Third, set an appointment with your creditors and request for a plan through which you can pay your debt appropriately. It is best to consult them in establishing the plan so that you can pay your debt in an effective way.

Fourth, you can ask for counseling from various organizations in order to improve your bad credit rating. These organizations can carry out negotiations with your creditors by convincing the latter to lower the interest rate and create a repayment plan for you.

Fifth, make sure to inform your creditors in advance if you are going to skip a repayment. However, it is best to avoid skipping payments since it would not always be in your favor.

Finally, make sure you are determined to follow the repayment plan that your creditor has provided for you. It is best not to play around with your creditors, especially when they have given you the chance to repay your debt in the most convenient way.

Important Steps to Take Towards Credit Repair

By now, you should already know how credit serves as an important tool in your life. For one, there are many things that having a good credit rating allows you to have. These include being able to rent a house or property, having a credit card, and qualifying for in-store financing among others. When you have a poor credit rating, it is advisable to take the necessary steps for to repair it. However, the process of repairing credit is usually slow and necessitates for rebuilding your credit rating over time. Fortunately, there are some tips that you can follow to start the credit repair process as soon as possible.

One, you can add accounts to your credit report. As discussed in the previous chapters, once you obtain a bad credit rating or denied for credit, make sure to obtain your credit report immediately from the credit bureau responsible for your account. Then, check for errors or discrepancies. If there are none, this means your credit rating is "poor" because your credit history is insufficient to reflect a good rating and not due to outstanding debts.

There are types of credit that credit bureaus do not tracked. These credit types usually come from small organizations. For instance, department store cards or gas cards are not included in your credit report. If you add these accounts to your credit report, you can rebuild a good credit rating. Thus, you should ask the concerned credit bureau to track these accounts. However, most credit bureaus ask for additional service fee when adding types of credit from small organizations. Only verifiable accounts are usually tracked by credit bureaus and added to your file free of charge.

Two, you can seek the help of a credit counsellor. When you become entangled in debt, it can be difficult to come out of it, especially if it has already fed on itself. This means that your original debt amount has gone higher due to its interest. Furthermore, if you find it taxing to carry out a credit repair on your own or continually encounter problems during the process of credit repair, you should consult a credit counselling agency.

There is a huge difference between a credit counseling company and a credit repair company. Credit counseling companies are non-profit services that offers guidance and advice on how to do a credit repair, while credit repair companies are for-profit organizations that charge fees for taking steps for repairing your credit; however, these steps are not necessarily legal or particularly conscious about ethics.

You can tell if you have found a good credit counsellor when he/she is able to make a realistic budget in which you can stick to as well as help in making practical decisions about your debts.

By adding accounts to your credit report and consulting a credit counsellor as necessary, you can make the process of credit repair easy. Make sure that the account that you will add to your credit report are in good standing.

Keep in mind that it can take a long time to obtain a good credit rating and an extremely short period to destroy it. Once your credit rating is damaged, you need to accept that there is no quick way to repair it. You will be obliged to rebuild your good credit standing from scratch. As such, you need to avoid the promises of credit repair companies that they have quick and easy solutions for a fee. An intelligent and practical way of repairing your credit is to improve your budgeting as well as spending habits.

Credit Repair and Your Creditors

Contacting your creditors is one of the best options you can do if you have missed payments, resulting in a bad credit rating. For most people, dealing with their creditors is an embarrassment; as such, they avoid the calls and refuse to speak with the creditors. If you have the same mentality as these people, you are in for a long-term difficulty when it comes to your credit.

Repairing your credit is essential for reclaiming various economic opportunities such as obtaining a credit card, securing a loan, or even getting an in-store financing. One of the easiest thing to do to start the process of credit repair is contacting your creditor once you get into a debt problem. Keep in mind that credit repair depends on your credit report and your credit report depends on your creditor's decision to report your account to the credit bureau.

In many cases, creditors are open to discuss alternative payment solutions and schemes given that they are not inclined to pushing you away. When they push you away, they are likely to receive no payment at all. Rather, creditors are generally open to discuss new payment terms with you. As such, it is always advisable to contact your creditor so you can repair your credit faster than resorting to credit repair companies.

If you decide to contact your creditors, make sure you are ready to propose a payment scheme, which is practical and realistic not only for you, but also to your creditor. It is necessary to propose a payment scheme that you can stick to. If you let yourself go on default on your proposed payment scheme, your creditor will think that you are just buying time to avoid payment.

In terms of outstanding debts, keep in mind that it is your creditor's decision whether or not to report your missed payment to the credit bureau. Thus, you should do your utmost effort to convince your creditor not to report your non-payment.

It is, therefore, advisable to contact your creditor as early as possible and propose a realistic and practical payment scheme to repair your credit.

Dealing with Credit Bureaus

Today, where the economy is at its weak point, having a good credit is a necessary tool. This is because it allows you to obtain house loans, car loans, credit card, and other convenient financial services and instruments. You may be able to live without having a good credit. On the other hand, if you have a bad credit rating, you will be affected negatively throughout your life, especially if you are not going to do something about it.

A credit bureau is the key to your credit rating. In North America, there are a number of credit bureaus that handle both positive and negative reports from creditors in order to create credit reports for a specific person. If your credit rating or history is poor, it is important that you know how to deal with the credit bureau that handles your report.

You can discern the credit bureau that holds your file by looking at any rejection letter you received from a recent credit application. In this letter, you will find out the credit bureau that proved your rating, which resulted to the refusal of your credit application.

Then, you need to obtain your credit report or history, which you can do so free of charge, specifically if you were denied credit recently. Most organizations will tell you that there is a fee for getting a credit report; however, you should only pay for a credit report if you need to obtain a copy of it instantly. The credit bureau will provide you with a copy of your credit report online for a certain fee.

If you are dealing with the credit bureau that handles your file, keep in mind that it belongs in the business of collecting and selling information. As such, you should not provide them with any detail, which is not necessary legally. The only information that you can provide them is your name, legal address, and social security number, but only for the purpose of obtaining your report. The credit bureau may also request for a copy of your driver's license or social security card, especially if the address it has on your file is different from your current address. You can send them a latest copy of a bill to prove your current address.

The primary reason why you should be cautious when transacting with credit bureaus is that they are likely to own a number of collection agencies. Furthermore, if you have a problem with your credit, you should only provide as little information as possible so that they also have little to bother you with.

When you already have your credit report, make sure to check for any error or discrepancy. If you find anything that is questionable in your report, you can send the credit bureau a written request for them to investigate on the error. In general, the credit bureau has the burden of documenting anything that is included in your credit report. If the credit bureau fails to investigate on the error or neglects your request for an investigation within 30 days, the error should be removed.

The basic strategy of most credit repair companies is to challenge all negative items in a credit report while charging their clients with outrageous fees. If they see that the negative item is already a few years old, they would still charge the client with a fee to have it removed. Fact is, once the client sends a request to the credit bureau for an investigation and the negative item is not verifiable, it should be removed.

You need to educate yourself about the legal obligations of credit bureaus in order to have a successful credit repair process. Prior to dealing with them, make sure you know all the legal aspects so you would not end up paying for something that should not be charged with a fee. Remember, credit bureaus are also businesses and that they own many credit repair companies.

Chapter 6

Credit Repair through Debt Consolidation

While one's economic situation is different from another person, most people may be in some debt at a particular time. For instance, you may have small debts such as in-store financing or credit card bills while other may have large ones such as mortgages and loans. This translates that almost everyone is most likely dependent on having a specific amount of credit. This is because credit can be useful for a number of things.

As mentioned earlier, your credit report, which is held by a credit bureau, is significant to your credit status. The credit bureau will send you a notification when you are in default or missed payments to your creditors. Once you receive such notices, expect that you are in for a poor credit rating.

There are various steps involved in effective credit repair. These steps are particular to a situation of an individual. One of the most common steps that people in a bad credit situation take is debt consolidation.

If you are attempting to have your credit repaired, it is important act as quickly as possible. Once you miss out on payments to your creditors, your credit rating will be damaged almost immediately. However, if you continuously miss your payments, the more damaged your credit rating will be.

You might be one of the numerous people who get confused that credit is simply "good" or "bad" and once you are in trouble with a creditor, it is a futile effort to repair it. On the contrary, even if you are in a bad credit situation, credit repair enables you to pay off your debts the quickest way possible. However, most people avoid any credit repair strategies because first off, they do not have money to pay their debts. For instance, you may have a poor economic situation, which is why you missed out on your payments. This is the reason why debt consolidation is an efficient tool, which can help you in repairing your credit.

Debt consolidation, as the name implies, consolidates all of your debts into just one loan. This means that if you have outstanding debts from various creditors, you can secure a loan from just one company and use the loan amount to pay your outstanding debts. You will only make your payments on the single loan and single creditor/company.

Through debt consolidation, you will be able have flexibility when your debts are already unmanageable. While you would still owe the same amount of money, debt consolidation allows you to secure a loan over a long term in order to lower your monthly payments. Furthermore, debt consolidation allows you to improve your relationship with your creditors and paves the way for repairing your credit. Through debt consolidation, your creditors will report to credit bureaus that your debts are already cleared up; thus, the credit repair process can start quickly.

Ultimately, debt consolidation changes your status with your creditors in a quick manner. It stops the damage to your financial situation before it gets worse. You can be on good terms with just a single creditor as compared to being on bad terms with multiple ones. In addition, debt consolidation allows you to breathe prior to engaging in credit repair.

Chapter 7

Credit Repair through Collections Agents

Time and again, it is mentioned in this book that credit ratings are based on credit reports. Once you loan from a bank, credit card companies, or other financial institutions, they report your status to a credit bureau, including your terms of payment, your timeliness in making your payments, etc. In turn, the credit bureau records any information provided to them into a credit report, which serves as the key to your credit rating.

Unfortunately, once you obtain negative markets on your credit crating, it will remain in your credit report for 7 years. This will prevent you from securing most types of loans. Your creditor will carry out different steps to make you pay your debt once you miss out on payments, regardless if it is a loan, financing, or credit card debt. More often than not, creditors give notices or warnings for a long period. Eventually, though, they will sell your debt to a collections agency. In this case, your creditors write-off the loan efficiently given that they are selling your debt at a huge discount.

Once your creditors decide that they have small chances of recovering the loan from you, they will take the loss by selling your debt to a collections agency even by half of the loan amount. As they do this, you will be reported to the credit bureau, leaving you with the lowest possible mark that will affect your credit rating for 7 years.

One signicant step to repairing your credit is to avoid making your creditors write-off your debt. When you are contacted by a collections agent, make sure you act as soon as possible. First, you should contact your creditor and see if you can make arrangements to clear your debt with them. More often than not, when you agree to pay the debt at once, the creditor will remove the mark, "gone to collection" from your credit rating, which is necessary for a quick credit repair. However, if your creditor does not agree with this arrangement, you have no choice but to stick with the collections agency.

At this point, your debt is already handed to a collections agency and that the negative mark on your credit report cannot get any worse than it already is. As such, you need to take into consideration your options for credit repair.

In general, the collections agent will demand aggressively that you pay the debt immediately and in full. He/she will also imply that you will be taken to court if you refuse to pay at once. When this happens, keep in mind that the collections agency has already bought your debt at, more or less, half its value. Thus, when you pay higher than that, the collections agency will profit.

If your circumstances would allow, you can offer the collections agency an arrangement that you will pay immediately less than half of your debt's full value. In many cases, the collections agent will try to close your file in order to avoid extending the process. Such an arrangement is usually accepted by most collections agencies.

If you want to repair your credit as soon as possible, it is best to pay your creditor instead of the collections agency. However, if your financial status would not allow you to do so, make an offer to the agency to lower the figure rather than paying the full loan amount. Keep in mind that paying a collections agency in full should be your last resort.

Chapter 8

Credit Repair through Credit Counseling

It would take a great deal of skill in order to master the are of budgeting. Some people may be better than others when it comes to managing their finances as well as maintaining a good credit standing. If you have any type of debt from a creditor or financial institution, it is best to learn how to manage your debt properly. This way, apart from keeping a good credit standing, you will also be allowed to secure credit when you need one in the future. On the other hand, if you miss out on payments towards your debts or allow them to go in default, you will be stuck with a negative mark, robbing you of economic opportunities.

If you want to repair your credit, it is essential to build up your credit rating again. One way of doing this is to consult or seek help from a credit counselor. More often than not, non-profit agencies carry out credit counseling. Some people confuse them with for-profit credit repair agencies, which often have a negative reputation due to scams, specifically those companies that advertise online. Other for-profit companies that are not scams are likely inclined to doing nothing that you cannot do on your own. For instance, they will simply instruct you to get a copy of your credit report and challenge any mistake on it. Some may even lead you to doing illegal activities such as obtaining a "new" credit rating by using a different address.

One of the most common problems with credit repair companies, which you should be aware of is they tend to propose a quick, one size fits all solution to any type of credit situation. Thus, if you encounter someone who claims he/she can fix your credit quickly without knowing about your credit situation is definitely not being truthful.

On the contrary, credit counseling services are there to provide you with advice regarding your attempt for credit repair. Consulting a credit counsellor is said to be the best way to do for people who want to repair their credit. This is because credit counselors can provide long term decisions and plans for efficient credit repair. They can also provide you with workshops and educational materials that help in understanding your credit as well as repairing it. Most credit counseling companies help people to learn creating and sticking to a budget, which can be beneficial for credit rating over the long term. In addition, these companies usually carry out one-on-one counseling for their clients so that they can learn and analyze one's credit situation. Consequently, they can provide the best economic decisions based on a specific credit status.

Credit counsellors are crucial in providing a specific kind of attention, which most credit repair companies tend to avoid. If you decide to seek the help of credit counsellors for repairing your credit, the solutions will usually be for a long term given that you will be taught how to manage and control your budget efficiently. Furthermore, you will also learn how to deal with permanent changes when it comes to your spending habits. By far, using a credit counseling company is most preferred when it comes to repairing credit.

Chapter 9

Do-It-Yourself Credit Repair

Some people find it easier to reestablish a good credit rating through "do-it-yourself credit repair." Each time you miss a payment, your creditor will report this to a credit bureau. The credit bureau will then add your missed payment record to your credit report. It gets worse when you miss payments too often or simply allow your loans to go into default. Your credit report will turn into chaos as you will be regarded as having a bad credit standing. When this happens, credit card companies will turn you down consistently as well as other types of loans. As such, you will need to repair your credit.

The previous chapters have discussed different ways to repair your credit. You can resort to debt consolidation, collections agencies, or credit counseling. You may even find various offers from different companies offering credit repair services on the classified ads or the internet. Most of these companies may be extremely aggressive in promoting their services. For instance, they may claim to fix your credit report for a certain fee. Therefore, you should be cautious when dealing with them given that most of these companies are scams. In addition, you can engage your credit repair more efficiently by yourself.

While most, if not, all credit repair companies imply that they can repair your credit situation, you should know that there is nothing they can do that you cannot do on your own. For instance, credit repair companies cannot have the poor marks on your credit report erased because they are not in any way in connivance with credit bureaus. What they are most likely to do is simply urge you to secure your credit report and challenge any error or discrepancy on it.

There are also some cases wherein credit repair companies resort to activities that are questionable in a legal aspect. They may urge you to "create" a "new" credit rating by changing your banking information as well as your address. Apart from being illegal, this practice is ineffective. If these are the only services that credit repair companies can offer, a better option is to do credit repair by yourself.

In a do-it-yourself credit repair, you can start by searching online for a step by step advice from government sources or trusted organizations. In general, you will be advised to secure your credit report from the concerned credit bureau. Then, you will be asked to examine your report thoroughly and challenge whatever errors you see on it. You will be advised to make a written complaint about the specific error to the concerned credit bureau. Make sure that you only challenge items that you know are genuine mistakes. If your credit report is free from mistakes or discrepancies, you will be asked to go through the traditional process of credit repair.

For instance, you will probably be advised to obtain a secured credit card, which you should use regularly. This way, you will be able to improve your credit rating slowly.

You will be able to pay creditors on a timely manner by making a smart budgeting plan, being careful on your spending habits, and being patient. Consequently, you will be able to prove creditors that you are worthy for credit.

While this manner of credit repair is a slow one, it is proven to be effective. Moreover, it is far more efficient and successful in the long term than obtaining the services of credit repair companies.

Chapter 10

Considering a Credit Repair Company

Almost everyone has a sort of debt such as a credit card balance, mortgage or car payments, or an outstanding home or student loan, which may all result in a credit history. Unfortunately, most people do not pay too much attention to their credit history until they are already in a poor credit standing. Your credit history has a significant effect in your life. If you have a poor credit history, you will not be able to obtain services without deposits, rent cars, or obtain a credit card. If you are in this situation, you need to engage in credit repair, as having a poor credit history is overwhelming and taxing.

More often than not, people with poor credit history are tempted to get involved in numerous companies offering a quick fix for bad credit for a certain fee. While most credit repair companies may be useful, many people find it unnecessary to transact with these companies. For one, they rarely do anything that you cannot do by yourself. They only imply that credit repair is an extremely difficult process that you cannot do on your own and that they are the only ones who can help you.

In general, most credit repair companies will ask you to obtain a copy of your credit report from the concerned credit bureau or reporting agency. Then, they will ask you to challenge the report for errors or mistakes in writing. It does not necessarily mean that there are indeed mistakes in your credit report. Most credit repair companies will urge you to take advantage of the credit bureau by imposing its legal obligation to conduct an investigation on your report and respond within 30 days. If the credit reporting agency fails to respond, especially if you are challenging multiple items, it will be obliged to remove the items in question from your report.

Although this strategy may seem effective initially, you should keep in mind that the credit bureau has the option to put back the removed items into your credit report once they have the proper documentation. This means that even if the credit bureau was not able to respond within 30 days due to lack of documentation, it will still continue investigating. Once they find the documentation for the questionable item, it will be put back into your credit report.

You should also be careful when dealing with credit repair companies as most of them are scams. It may be too late for you to discover that a credit repair company is a scam given that these types of companies are bound to provide all promised services prior to accepting payment. In addition, these companies are obliged to present an outline of all the services and fees they will provide. Should you decide to take the services of a credit repair company, it is advisable to read and understand all the fine print and paperwork they provide.

Chapter 11

Secured Credit Cards for Credit Repair

People who have no credit rating are those who never paid a monthly bill, taken out a loan, or had a credit card. Perhaps these people are minors or children who depend on their parents or others for their finances. However, for those who own a house, have a credit card, or taken out a loan, it is impossible for them not to have a credit rating.

As mentioned frequently in this book, if you owe money to a creditor, your payments, whether or not they are timely will be reported to a credit bureau or reporting agency, which compiles your credit file. Us, if you miss out on payments, say, on a loan or credit card, you will receive a negative mark on your file or credit rating. Moreover, if your creditor sends your outstanding debt to a collections agency, all the more that you will be prevented from obtaining credit in the future due to a poor credit rating. In the event that you are in one of these situations, you need to engage in credit repair.

If you choose not to do anything, you will have a negative credit rating for up to seven years, which will surely cause more troubles, especially if you want to obtain any kind of loan. Fortunately, one of the most efficient ways to repair your credit is to acquire a secured credit card.

In general, when you are in a bad credit situation, you will be rejected from applying any credit card. Consequently, you will be put in a circumstance wherein you have no other way of improving your credit rating in terms of proving that you can actually pay your bills responsibly and on time.

On the other hand, the secured credit card is a type of credit card that is offered specifically to people with a poor credit rating. In general, a secured credit card works by depositing an amount that is equal to the credit limit. For instance, if you deposit $1,000 initially, your credit limit will be $1,000. The issuer or company of the credit card has the right to use your initial deposit upon any outstanding balance should you fail to make payments after a specific period. As such, there would be no risk for the issuer or company of the credit card given that they can use your initial deposit against your balance. On your part, you will not end up owing the issuer or company anything. These are the reasons why secured credit cards are issued freely to individuals, especially those with bad credit rating. However, you would have to pay annual fees to keep a secured credit card, which regular credit cards do not require.

When you already have a secured credit card, you can start repairing your credit by using the card regularly. Make sure that you make timely payments to show creditors that you can be trusted with credit. This way, you can repair your credit in a slow but efficient manner. In addition, using your secured credit card can reduce the seven-year period prior to being granted credit again.

Chapter 12

Credit Repair, Bad Credit Loans and Mortgage Options

Today, many people are involved in a type of loan, which is already considered as a part of daily life. When you are in need of a loan and you have a poor credit rating, you will be denied by creditors based on your file from credit bureaus. In order to overcome this type of problem, you can obtain bad credit loans that are often offered by credit companies, banks, and other financial institutions.

There are various reasons why many people have credit problems. Some may be deprived from jobs for a long time or some kind of unemployment problem. Others may have insufficient savings to pay for their debts. Fortunately, most companies and financial organizations offer bad credit loans for people who are in a bad credit situation.

Bad credit loans can help in sustaining a stable financial state as well as saving one from being denied for a loan. The most common type of bad credit loan is bad debt consolidation. Nowadays, many companies offer online service of debt management for bad credit. This online service helps in getting rid of debts, improving credit score, and strengthening credit.

If you want to apply for a bad credit loan, make sure to avoid the creditors, financial companies, or lenders that you have already borrowed money from. They may offer debt consolidation for bad credit; however, they will be cautious when offering you their services given that you already have a bad record. Thus, it is advisable to secure a bad credit loan from a new creditor or financial company that can offer you better options to improve your credit rating.

If your debt is solely due to credit cards, you can opt for a credit card debt consolidation. This type of bad credit loan can help you in integrating the remaining balances on your credit cards into a single credit card or big loan. More often than not, the interest rate on this credit card debt consolidation is less than your current loan.

Keep in mind that a scheme for credit card debt consolidation merges all your outstanding debts into just one loan with less interest rate. You can also shift your blance to a credit card scheme with a zero interest rate. As much as possible, repay your credit card earlier than the due date to avoid additional expenses on interest.

Credit Repair and Unsecured Loans

Due to the developments in the loan markets, you will be relieved of your worries about your bad credit rating, especially if you are in need of extra cash. Today, people with poor credit rating do not have to feel like it is the end of the world. Creditors and other financial institutions now offer unsecured loans, which are specifically designed for people with poor credit scores or bad credit rating.

When unsecured loans were first conceptualized, they were premeditated for borrowers who do not have any collateral, valued asset, or property to pledge. These unsecured loans also have the features of a secured loan; however, they offer more flexibility for borrowers with bad credit rating.

Although bad credit unsecured loans have high high interest rates, you will not be required to provide a collateral. The high interest rate is only for an added security on the part of the loaning company. In general, the interest rates of bad credit unsecured loans range from 12% to 20%. Furthermore, the interest rates may change depending on the credit rating of the borrower, the actual loan amount, and the capacity of the borrower to repay. The total loan amount you can get from a bad credit unsecured loan can be as much as $25,000.

Given that there is no collateral needed, the process of getting an unsecured loan for poor credit is faster than regular or secured loans. Creditors or financial institutions offering unsecured loans may only require minimum documents to start the process.

Once you receive your loan amount, you can use it for various purposes such as funding a vacation, purchasing new furniture, starting a small business, financing a wedding, or consolidating debts from other loans.

On the other hand, even if the features of bad credit unsecured loans may seem lucrative, you still need to be cautious, especially on your capability to repay the amount along with its interest. Prior to applying for a bad credit unsecured loan, it is advisable to scout for a number of loaning companies and checkout their policies. This way, you will feel relaxed and safe knowing that you will be dealing with a reputable company.

Due to the increasing number of creditors and loan agencies offering bad credit unsecured loan, it is becoming common these days to get one. Thus, you need to be cautious about the competitive loan schemes offered. Make sure that the deals would suit your needs, requirements, and capability to repay. You should also pay attention to the terms and conditions imposed by the creditor, making sure it does not go against your actual purpose or need for getting the loan.

Credit Repair and Mortgage Options

If you are one of the numerous people who dream of purchasing a new home or the latest four-wheeler, but cannot do so due to lack of funds or have a bad credit, then you should keep reading.

Back in the days, creditors or lenders completely block or reject clients who are in a bad credit situation. There were no options offered. However, with the changing times, creditors or lenders now offer a number of options to attract potential clients or borrowers whether or not they are in a bad credit situation.

If you are planning to obtain a credit finance with bad credit, you should consider certain factors including average deals, credit score, two-type mortgage facility, and rebuild credit.

When it comes to mortgage deals, you should expect that the best deals are for people who have good credit ratings. As such, avoid going for a mortgage if you expect to be given a good loan deal in spite of your bad credit rating. On the other hand, there are fair loan deals that are offered to help you with your financial status.

For instance, a zero down loan finance offers freedom from property pledging or any form of security. However, this depends on your credit score. With the required legal documents, you can obtain a mortgage amount even if you have a low credit score of 600.

You should also consider the two-type mortgage facility, which is the 75/25 or 85/15. This mortgage facility offers rates that allow you to save as well as discard the need for any form of insurance.

When it comes to mortgage security, you can obtain a secured loan despite having a poor credit rating as long as you have a real estate or property under your name. This will definitely entice creditors given the value of your asset. In addition, creditors would be risk-free if you offer them a sort of security.

There are traditional mortgage systems that allow you to obtain credit even if you have a bad credit rating. However, these mortgage systems may offer higher interest rates than regular mortgages. Thus, you need to choose the right mortgage deal that suits you best.

Prior to applying a loan for a new home or car, make sure to rebuild your credit, improving your credit score, or making it higher. Although it may take a while before you can purchase a new home or car, it is worth your effort to rebuild your credit. It may also be an advantage by the time you are already qualified for a regular loan given that you can get a better deal with a lower rate of interest and a large loan amount.

Finally, if you are up for a mortgage deal, make sure to analyze it carefully. The tendency of most people who are in a bad credit situation is to simply engage in a mortgage deal without understanding the conditions of the creditor. This is because they are desperate to take the loan regardless if it includes high interest rates. You should not let this happen. Only sign contracts for a mortgage deal if you have already studied and analyzed the conditions thoroughly. Make sure you have ample time to read the agreement papers and find out if there are any pitfalls, which you might regret later.

Remember that there are various types of mortgage loans available. These include flexible payment schemes, fixed interest rates, and low interest rates among others. There are also online sites that provide good deals with relevant information on their offers. However, if you are planning to look for creditors online, make sure to check their reputation prior to signing a mortgage deal. Nevertheless, be it online or offline, there are numerous mortgage options being offered even if you have a poor credit rating.

Credit Repair and Bad Credit Car Financing

By now, you should have already realized that bad credit is the same as poor credit scoring. "Bad credit" is a term used for an individual who has a credit record due to non-payment of bills, mortgages, loans, and/or services on time. A person regarded as a bad credit is considered a high risk for creditors, banks, and other financial institutions.

In a layman's point of view, bad credit simply means the ineligibility to obtain loans with appropriate or fitting interest rates. Consequently, if you are planning to purchase a car by obtaining a loan while you are in a bad credit situation, you should consider some factors first.

You should always keep in mind, specifically when you want to get credit that being in a bad credit situation entails a number of negative effects. For one, you would surely be rejected for a car loan application. You could also be charged with high interest rate. Even the car seller might offer you a vehicle that has a higher price than the actual price.

While creditors or lenders may approve your car loan application in spite of your bad credit rating, it does not mean that you have fulfilled your dream of having a new car. You still need to repay the amount you loaned as well as the interest rate that comes with the loan. People who have good credit rating can obtain a car finance with a low interest rate of 10% and a loan term of up to 7 years.

You can also obtain a car finance with an interest rate of 5% to 26% while the loan term can be just 2 to 4 years. You may also be required to pay a down payment of up to 50% of the total price of the car. As such, you need to analyze the solution.

If you are in a bad credit situation, you need to accept the fact that obtaining a car finance is inappropriate. However, if you are in dire need of a new car, you should discern whether or not you are willing and capable to pay a high interest rate. You also need to determine if you are willing to let go of a huge part of your income just to pay for a new car on a monthly basis.

Based on the different experiences of people with bad credit who obtained a car finance, the best solution to avoid the negative effects is not to get a car loan at all. If you are in a bad credit situation, you should head in the direction of ameliorating your credit rating instead of risking another loan that could result in worse effects. While you still have a negative mark on your credit report, you should learn to manage your finances effectively and make sure to repay your debts on time. Keep in mind that improving your credit rating may take several months. Make your dream of having a new car your motivation to improve your credit score at the soonest possible time.

Credit Repair and Financing a Computer

It may be surprising to learn that even people with high-salaried jobs or those who are able to pay their bills and rentals on time are declined from obtaining a loan. The primary reason for this may be a missing credential credit rating on their part. Other reasons may include bankruptcy or a sudden descent in their careers. If you are in a similar situation, it may be difficult to obtain a loan or funding from lenders. More so, if you are planning to purchase a new computer or gadget, you may also experience problems due to lack of financing.

These days, technology and the economic condition have progressed to higher levels. This is evident in the loan markets with positive transitions in doing their business. In the past, people were hesitant to come out and obtain a loan from lenders. Part of this is due to the strict policies of creditors and financial institutions. Today, however, even wealthy individuals and influential companies take out loans as creditors now offer reasonable monthly installments and easier payment methods. Even those with bad credit ratings and default bank statements are allowed to obtain certain loans. Loans have become possible to obtain due to the huge number of creditors, loan companies, and financial institutions that provide sensible loan deals.

If you are in a bad credit situation and want to purchase a new computer or gadget through financing, you can do so through various ways. One, you can obtain a personal loan. When you decide to take on a personal loan, make sure that you do so from a reputable creditor or bank. If you have a mortgage property, it would be easier for you to obtain a personal loan. Personal loans are considered as the most popular loan given that they are easy to get. Thus, it is a sure way to get that dream computer or gadget regardless if you are in a bad credit situation.

Two, you can rent a computer, especially if you need one for immediate use. However, renting a computer should be your last resort. You can also look for deals wherein you rent to own the equipment. More often than not, the scheme for rent-to-own is paying two to three times the computer's original value; however, you may have to settle with a used or second-hand one.

Three, you can look for computer retail companies that have a lay away option. If you are badly in need of a computer, purchasing a new one may take 90 days, specifically if you buy it through financing. If you are able to provide income within a certain period in spite of your bad credit situation, computer companies with lay away schemes may offer you their deal.

Fourth, there are computer agencies that grant financing loans to their customers when buying a computer. However, you need to present them with valid documents that will discern your financial credibility. Most computer dealers allow customers to pay with advance cheques, especially those in a bad credit situation.

While arranging for finance if you have a bad credit rating is quite difficult, it is still possible. However, you should remember that the value of the computer you would purchase through financing would be higher than its actual value. Naturally, it would be a different story if you have a good credit rating or just enough to purchase a computer in a normal way. Then again, you should look at the brighter side. When you purchase a computer through financing, it can ameliorate your credit rating as long as you pay on time and that you pay the full amount due. Therefore, keep your tension away as with the proper loan deals, you would be able to get your dream computer model through financing despite your bad credit situation.

Chapter 13

Credit Repair and Bad Credit Cards

If you are one of the numerous individuals who are worried about their bad credit history, you can rely on bad credit cards to help you improve your credit rating.

Bad credit cards are one of the most preferred ways in maintaining a good credit score level. Both consumers and merchants have discerned that bad credit cards are efficient tools for credit cardholders who are regarded as high-risk. This is because these credit cards serve as a regular credit card even if the cardholder has a credit rating of 550 or below.

More often than not, people in a bad credit situation opt for prepaid debit cards, secured credit cards, and other bank cards given that normal credit cards are not available for them. However, if you have a bad credit rating, you can avail of bad credit cards just like regular credit cards. Even if bad credit cards have higher interest rates and lower credit limits, it is advisable to get one and use it to improve your credit rating.

Most people who are in a bad credit situation have various misconceptions about bad credit cards. For one, many people think that these cards are not an effective financial backup. However, these misconceptions are unwarranted. Today, bad credit cards are no longer regarded as bad financial tools. This is because not all of these cards come with outrageous interest rates. In fact, there are a number of financial companies that have decent offers in terms of annual fees, financing fees, credit necessities, opening offers, and online banking accessibility among others.

If you only look past the low credit limit and high interest rate, you will find that bad credit cards have many benefits. Apart from helping you improve your credit score, these cards can assist you in becoming a low-risk borrower as time passes by. However, make sure that your circumstance allows you to pay off the balance in a timely manner.

Furthermore, bad credit cards can help in securing your chances of getting a loan in the future. This can be achieved by using these cards for small purchases for at least a year or two. Consequently, you will be able to rebuild your credit rating while impressing the creditors of your good credit score.

Bad credit cards can be your best friend, especially if you have a bad credit history. Keep in mind that these cards can help repair your credit as well as improve your prospective for obtaining a loan in the future.

Credit Repair and Corporate Credit

Finance is one of the most important factors when it comes to establishing and growing a business. Every business is geared towards getting loans in order to comply with its needs and requirements. Back in the days, most businessmen obtain credit with their private properties as their collateral. This entails a high risk given that the success of a business can never be guaranteed. This situation paved the way to the idea of corporate credit, which became a prominent term for a short period.

Corporate credit is an unsecured loan, which is funded by commercial organizations. The credit history of the borrower is the only basis for granting this type of loan. As such, there is no risk of losing your personal properties or assets. However, if you have a bad credit rating, there is a little difference when obtaining corporate credit, specifically if you are establishing a business.

To obtain a corporate credit, it is best to declare your business as an LLC. This means that it is best to register your business as an

LLC in order build its reputation easily in the market. More often than not, businesses with a a proprietorship status is judged from the credibility of its owner. Therefore, if you have a bad credit history, it would be difficult to obtain a business loan. However, if you register your business as an LLC, the process of obtaining a corporate credit is smoother and your business is not judged from your poor credit rating, but from its own reputation.

When applying for a corporate credit, it is advisable to make your business accessible by adding little details such as its commercial phone line and physical address. This way, creditors and clients will find your business easy to reach. In addition, make sure you secure all requirements such as excellent rating from bank, sufficient number of trade references, running license, and DUNS number among others.

It is also wise to purchase materials for your business through trade credit. Given that you are in a bad credit situation and probably in a poor financial state, it is unwise to purchase distinct business requirements by paying cash.

By registering your business as an LLC to the creditor or financial organization, you can obtain a fair corporate credit. In the past, only owners of businesses with a credit score of 640 and above were granted corporate credit. This is because they grant credit based on the owners' credit rating. Today, creditors, lenders, and other financial institutions already grant corporate credit even to those who have bad credit history. By establishing your own business and registering it as an LLC, you will find various corporate loans being offered despite having a bad credit rating.

Chapter 14

Credit Repair and Loan Problems

Some people with bad credit ratings cannot help but plunge in various offers from lenders such as a mortgage for home improvements or a lucrative house deal. If you are one of these people who would easily plunge into such deals, there are factors that you should consider.

You need to find the right creditor or lender who could offer your property the best value as well as finance you appropriately. If you are in a bad credit situation, the lender will assess your credit rating and monthly income in order to determine your loan amount. If the lender allows you to loan a huge amount, it is advisable to have a short period for repayment. It is better to have a 12- to 15-year repayment period for your mortgage loan than a 20- to 25 year loan term.

Ask for various loan schemes to discern the one that suits you best. Some loan schemes allow you to repay in thirty years with a fixed monthly installment. There are also loan schemes with low rates of interest. Numerous credit finance programs offer protection or a rate cap that you may need to prevent changes in the interest rate. Some loan schemes also allow you to pay up the interest rate of your loan amount for a limited period. When you are looking for the right lender and deal, make sure to discern the true value of your property as well as the costs that you might be charged with.

Based on standard rules and regulations, creditors or lenders are required to furnish a financial statement of your loan sanction within 3 to 4 days. Furthermore, if the down payments are no more than 20% of the loan amount, you are entitled for a private mortgage insurance. If you are applying for secured loans, you may submit your application several times. This is because the rates of interest may increase depending on the current business economy and the market. Rates of interest may increase due to inflation.

Keep in mind that any amount of financing or funding that you receive from a creditor or financial institution will be reflected in your credit report. In order to discern the down payment of a loan amount, the creditor or lender will assess the credibility of future borrowers from properties under their name, monthly income statements, and equity shares that they hold. If you are planning a garden landscaping or make home improvements, you can avail of standard mortgage loans once you have repaired your bad credit. If you think you will need home painters, electricians, and building contractors, you can avail of a construction loan to pay these workers for their jobs.

The good news is even if you are in a bad credit situation, you can obtain a loan amount easily due to the flourishing loan markets today.

Chapter 15

How To Get Your Credit Reports

As promised, this chapter will tell you about getting your free credit report and the places from where you can get yours.

One of the most significant things to determine your economic status is your credit rating. If you have a good credit rating, there will be no hassles in getting loans, credit cards, and mortgages among others. However, if you have missed out on payments with a creditor, expect that the creditor will report such noncompliance to the credit bureau or reporting agency. The credit bureau will then place a negative mark on your credit report.

If you have a bad credit rating, you should keep in mind that most doors will be closed, specifically in the financial world. For instance, you would not be able to get almost all types of loans. You would not be able to shop online given that you do not have a credit card. You would not be able to rent a car if you need one. All these reasons direct you towards repairing your credit at the soonest possible time. To start a credit repair, you need to obtain your credit report from the concerned credit bureau or reporting agency.

In the United States and Canada, only a handful of credit bureaus is available, making it easy for one to discern which holds his/ her credit report. In the event that you applied for a credit card and were turned down, the "rejection" letter of the creditor would indicate the credit reporting agency that holds your report. Keep in mind that it is your right to get a copy of your credit report without being charged of fees.

To request for your credit report, simply visit the website of the credit bureau or reporting agency and download the application. Fill it up and mail it together with your photocopied identification card to the agency. The credit bureau should be able to send you the credit report you requested in a timely manner.

More often than not, credit bureaus allow individuals to view their credit history online; however, there is a fee that comes along with it. Regardless if you choose to request your through mail or view it online, your credit report is the first step to repairing your credit.

Once you have obtained your credit report, it is important to examine it thoroughly. Look for any inaccuracy or mistake in your report. In the event that there is an inaccuracy, you need to request from the agency to have it investigated. It is likewise your right to have the inaccuracy investigated; as such, you should not hesitate doing so. Once you have requested for an investigation on a particular item in your credit report, the credit bureau should respond within 30 days. It should be able to provide the documentation for the item you are questioning. If the credit bureau fails to respond within 30 days, the item should be removed or deleted from your report.

If you are requesting for an investigation on a particular item in your report, it is advisable to send the credit bureau any supporting document when available. In some cases, credit bureaus confuse your information with another individual with the same name as yours. Credit bureaus also tend to make outright errors on your credit report. In addition, during the process of investigation, you may also request the credit bureau to have the item marked as "under investigation."

While it may seem to be a taxing process, it is necessary to obtain your credit report to begin your credit repair. If you do not known anything about your credit history, it is impossible to know where you truly stand apart from being in a bad credit situation. Ultimately, you need to find out how bad your credit is as well as the reason for being regarded as "bad credit."

For instance, you need to find out the reason for your bad credit rating is a single outstanding debt or multiple debts. You need to know how long the item has been in your credit report as well as how long it will remain in your credit history. These are essential things that you need to know so that you can start the process of credit repair efficiently.

According to the law, you have a right to receive a copy of your credit report every year from each of the three credit reporting companies; this is free. These three companies have joined efforts to provide a seamless service through a central website, a mailing address and a toll free telephone number where you can call to request your free annual report. So, essentially, you don't have to contact each credit bureau separately to get your free report. This means that you can use any of the three options available:

> 1 Request the report online at https://www.annualcreditreport.com/index.action, the website I mentioned above. The report will be available instantly.

> 2 Download a request form here http://www.consumer.ftc.gov/articles/pdf-0093-annual-report-request-form.pdf then mail it to *Annual Credit Report Request Service.* Expect your report within 15 days.

> 3 Call the toll free number 1-877-322-8228 to request your free report; it will be mailed to you within 15 days.

Note: You can order/request your free annual credit report from each of the 3 nationwide credit bureaus at the same time or at different times. This will help you understand if you have the same kind of report from each of these bureaus.

These places are established to help you out and it will be useless if you don't take their help. You must call for your reports from them and go through it to understand where you stand and whether there are mistakes in your report. Your credit score needs to be fixed at any cost and for this, you must put in some efforts. Even if it is not your fault for having a low score, you must not let the companies get away with cheating you and fight for what is your right.

As is apparent, it only takes a call or typing in a little information. Should not take you any more than 5 or 10 minutes and you will be happy to have taken care of something so important. You will have access to your reports within a matter of a fortnight. Once you get it, go through it thoroughly. Don't think there will be good news coming your way as not checking your reports for a long time will cause you to find a lot of errors and erroneous entries. You will find several mistakes and might need to sit with a pen to circle each of these. You will need some of your own records to match it with whatever is mentioned in the report. This will make it easier for you to find the loop holes in the credit report.

Once you are done finding the mistakes, you need to deduct them and look at the score that you can actually reach. You might be shocked to see a considerate increase in your score and something that will catapult you to the average or good score range. If you are having problems interpreting your report and not understanding what is what then don't worry. The next chapter is dedicated to this topic alone and will tell you how you can interpret your report and understand the various elements that are mentioned on your credit report card.

Many times, a bad credit score can wreak havoc in your life. You will have a different picture in mind but the reality will turn out to be something else. Once you make the effort to collect your credit report, you must dedicate at least an entire day to make sense of it and look for errors. It might sound daunting but needs to be done at any cost. Once you find out what is causing you your bad score you can immediately deal with it by making use of the prescribed methods.

In as much as the free reports are available to everyone every year, you need to follow up with what is reported in your report every year if you don't want surprises; the earlier you get things fixed on your report, the better for you. Imagine having some creditor report wrong information about a debt that you completely paid and on time. Will that be fair to you?

Similarly, there can be duplication and two or more creditors claiming the same charge. All of it will result in you having a low credit score and ruin your chances of availing credit at nominal interest rates. The best strategy here is to have a credit monitoring service that will help in monitoring whatever is happening on your account since you will be getting monthly credit reports. When looking for a credit monitoring service, you should look for a company that offers FICO scores since those that offer FAKO or simply credit score may give you a false sense of security. They might say one thing but the truth might be something else.

Perhaps I should explain that there is a difference between Credit Score (FAKO) and FICO Score. Most credit monitoring service providers will only provide a report of the credit score, which means that you wouldn't get the FICO score. Credit score scale goes up to 900 while the FICO score goes up to about 750. Most banks and other lending institutions use FICO score to determine your credit worthiness. You will be shocked to discover that your FICO score is way lower than you thought when your FAKO is converted to FICO. So if you have a credit score of 700, you might be shocked to discover that your sense of security is unfounded when your score is converted to FICO since it will probably be in the range of low-to-mid 600s.

This might cause you to panic and start doing the wrong things. Therefore, as a rule of thumb, you should enroll to a credit monitoring service that gives you FICO scores. This will probably be a premium service that you can expect to pay anywhere between $10 and $15 but it is worth every penny since your credit score has a profound effect on many things in your life.

You can avail your FICO score from any one of the major consumer reporting agencies namely TransUnion, Equifax PRBC or Experian. These will help you with your scores and familiarize you with your credit risk.

Now that you know how to source for good credit reports, what then after you have enrolled for the credit reporting services? When you receive the report, you need to interpret it correctly to help you identify anything that could taint your rating.

Chapter 16

How To Interpret The Credit Report

Enrolling for a credit monitoring service won't be the magic bullet that will make you have an error free credit report; you have to know what things you should be looking for in your credit report if you are to actually get to dispute anything derogatory. The best approach to use when interpreting all credit reports is to go through the specific sections in your credit report looking for individual items that could be derogatory. Let's go through some of the crucial sections to look at when reviewing your credit report:

Your personal profile

In this section, you will find your name, date of birth, your past and present addresses, your employers, personal information and aliases. You should look for incorrect names, addresses, aliases etc. You can file a dispute for anything that is incorrect, anything that is erroneous and anything that you don't want disclosed to everyone. Many people don't go through this column in detail as they won't think there will be any sort of an error here. But they will be shocked to find many errors and that these are causing them their bad scores. So go through your personal profile on a monthly basis and don't take it casually.

Inquiries

When you apply for any credit, the specific creditor will want to know your credit rating in order to make a decision on whether to approve or reject the application. They will also use this information to know how much interest to charge for the loan. The creditors will buy/request your credit report from the credit reporting agencies. Perhaps you should know that more results in this section within a short period, the worse of your credit rating will be. This is because the section shows your spending habits; creditors will mostly check this section before approving or declining credit. When you have a problem with this section, you can be sure that it will be easy to have it fixed since most creditors will probably not respond within the time allowed by the law.

Your account history
Your credit report will probably have a separate classification for all the items in your credit report such that accounts related to installment loans, real estate, public records, revolving funds etc are stated separately. It is very important to confirm that each of the entries in this section is accurate or properly stated. In essence, you should be looking at the creditor's name, past due amount, date opened, monthly payment, balance owed for different accounts and high balance just to mention a few.

You should also check to ascertain that the status that is showed on your credit reports is actually correct; check for open, unpaid, closed and in collection. Go through each and every aspect in detail and make sure that there are no errors anywhere. As soon as you spot one, quickly circle it so that you know where exactly the mistake lies. If you find anything that doesn't tally with what you know is the correct status, you can file a dispute.

As a rule of thumb, you should never overlook all the components in your credit report including the payment status since this adversely affects your score. Also, you should check your credit report for anything related to late payments in your payment history in the past 30, 60, 90 & 120 days. Since most reports usually color code this section, you should have it easy in trying to identify any derogatory items after which you can file a dispute.

The credit report summary

As the name suggests, this section gives a summary of the entire credit report. Although it is a summary, it doesn't mean that it isn't detailed. There will be plenty of detail in regard to your credit report. In fact, you will find a summary of accounts that have been closed, opened, debt in collections, real estate and debt outstanding among others. As a rule of thumb, scrutinize every item reported in this section for accuracy and validity.

You should also expect to note any discrepancies with other sections. You should, also check the derogatory items section in your credit report summary to ascertain such items like public records, present delinquencies and collection accounts are eliminated; you should work towards ensuring that you have more zeros in this section. All this might sound like it will considerably improve your score but you need to be alert and not jump to any conclusions.

As long as you are doing all the right things there will only be a positive impact on your credit report. Don't worry if you are taking a lot of time as it might take some time for you to understand whether you are doing the right thing. Don't be in a hurry to finish and spend some time fixing your credit report.

The public records

The items that you will find in this section include the judgments, bankruptcies and tax liens. I should point out that this section has a profound effect on your credit rating so ensure that what is reported here is correct. Therefore, you should file a dispute if anything in this section doesn't tally with your records. Again, spend a substantial amount of time going through each and every aspect mentioned here. Don't be too quick to jump the gun. Find out if there are indeed some key errors that can help you settle your case one and for all. The errors should be big enough for the bureau to take notice and help you fix it. There can be deliberate errors that are put in to make your credit worthiness look bad and you must put in efforts to have it rectified at the earliest, for your own benefit.

What next after you determine which items are derogatory? The next step is commencing the dispute process. For this, you need to follow a set pattern in order to avail the best possible results. The next chapter will explain the steps that you need to take in detail.

Chapter 17

The Dispute Process: What You Need To Know

Don't be too quick to file your dispute; you need to be tactful about the matter otherwise you might end up wasting too much time for nothing. Start by coming up with a list of the accounts you would want to dispute as you read through your credit report.

Armed with the list, start creating different dispute letters for all of the accounts. At this stage, you have 3 options on the approach to take in the dispute process.

➢ File your dispute online

➢ Visit the credit bureau's offices to file your dispute

➢ Send the dispute letter through email

If you opt to mail the letters, you should allow about 30-45 days for the dispute to be processed. Don't forget to have a sentence that indicates that the bureau should respond to you via mail. Once the 30-45 days are over, the response from the bureaus will include wordings like updated, verified, deleted and remains although some more information might also be available. If you are not satisfied with the response from the credit bureau, you can file another (unique dispute) for the same account. This is mostly done when the bureau has made up its mind to not show an interest in your dispute. You will know if they are doing things to dissuade you from pursuing your interests.

Take note that the last payment date on any account has a profound negative effect on your credit score. This date will determine the period within which a particular entry will show up in your credit report. So, in essence, you can compel a creditor to remove the derogatory item from your credit report if they want you to pay them the outstanding amount. This technique is called pay to delete and entails having the creditor update in your credit report that you have paid the outstanding amount; in this case, they promise to update on your report that you have $0 balance.

I know that this might look good when you don't know what it means but the truth is that it doesn't even improve your credit rating contrary to what collection companies will sometimes promise you in order to pay the outstanding debt. On the contrary, it taints your credit rating since it will stick there for 7 or more years. Other creditors will use that against you in evaluating whether you qualify for a credit and will even charge you more.

It is like the previous creditor is telling the other creditors to take caution when dealing with you so in essence, you will be a high risk borrower who has to pay more to access credit. If any positive improvement is to be noted, that entry has to be deleted from your credit report. Instead of tainting your credit rating even further by showing any effort to pay, you would rather let it expire after 7 years. As a rule of thumb, never give up in your quest to disputing any incorrect derogatory items in your credit report. Even when a creditor tries to validate the entry, look for something else to base your dispute on. As you do it consistently, you should probably start seeing these items disappearing from your credit report.

So, now that you understand the importance of doing everything right during the dispute process, the next question you should be asking yourself is what to have in your dispute letters. Here are a few things that MUST be in the dispute letter; the rest really don't count much in the dispute process as you will notice in the subsequent chapters.

⌑ ✐ Your first and last name spelt accurately

▤ ✐ Your SSN must be accurate

▤ ✐ Your driver's license must be there and accurately stated

▤ ✐ Include pay stub or W2 form that shows your name and your SSN number

▤ ✐ You need to have your current home address stated accurately

⌛ ✐ You must provide any other form of identification

Please note that a slight mistake in this section will probably result to your dispute being rejected. Additionally, don't just write your name in a bunch of letters. Instead, ensure that each letter has your account name, account number and the creditor's name in there. You should also look out for variations in account numbers for the same account; creditors are notorious for reporting different numbers in the three credit bureaus. Therefore, as a rule of thumb, be certain on the account number that you are disputing in a certain credit bureau.

Chapter 18

Effective Strategies For Repairing Your Credit

Pay to delete strategy

If you have derogatory items in your credit report, you can opt to pay the unpaid credit balance only if the creditor agrees to delete the items from your credit report. As I already mentioned, don't agree for a $0 balance appearing on your credit report since this taints your reputation. As a rule of thumb, less is more in this section; the fewer items you have here, the better off for you. This method works through the idea that your report doesn't show whether you have had any history of bad credit in the derogatory items section. This will ultimately improve your rating. Actually, the idea is to ensure that whatever amount you agree to pay doesn't show up as your last date of activity. If the creditor only cares about their money, why should they bother telling the world that you have finally paid?

In most instances, the creditors often write off debts within just 2 years of constant defaulting after which this information is sold in bulk to a collection company for some pennies of a dollar. This means that the collection companies will even be just fine if you even pay a fraction of what you ought to pay. Whatever you pay, they will still make money! This makes them open to negotiations such as pay to delete since they have nothing to lose anyway.

> ➢ Therefore, only use the pay to delete approach at this level and not any other. Actually, the only other way around it for the collection company is a judgment, which can be costly so you have some advantage here.

> ➢ Additionally, use this strategy when new negative items start showing up in your report that could hurt your reputation as a credit consumer.

> ➢ Also, since the creditors will often sell the same information to multiple collection companies, you might probably start noting the same debt being reported by several companies; use pay to delete to get them off your report.

> ➢ You can also use this strategy if you have not been successful in getting items off your credit report using other methods. This is opting to go the dispute way might only make the process cyclic, which will be cumbersome, tiresome and frustrating; you don't want to get into this cycle.

Now that you know when to use this method, understanding how the entire process works is very critical. To start with, ensure that you get an acceptance in writing if they agree to your times; don't pay without the letter! After you agree, allow about 45 days for next credit report to be availed to you by your credit monitoring service. These companies have the legal power to initiate the deletion process so don't accept anything less such as updating the balance; it is either a deletion or nothing. If they try to stall the process by saying that they cannot delete, mention that it will only take about 5 minutes for them to fill the Universal Data Form. Don't worry if one company seems not to agree with your terms since another one will probably show up and will gladly take the offer.

In any case, what do they have to gain when they keep your debt when you are willing to pay? Remember that the records will just be in your records for 7 years so since 2 years are already past, these companies have no choice otherwise you can simply let the 7 years to pass! *However, don't use this as an excuse for not paying your debts since the creditors can sue you to compel you to pay outstanding amounts.* The aim of this process is to ensure that whatever bad experience you have with one creditor doesn't make the others to make unfavorable decisions on your part.

NOTE: don't be overly aggressive with creditors who have a lot to lose in the process especially the recent creditors since they can probably sue you. Your goal is to only be aggressive with creditors that are barred by the statute of limitation from suing you in court. You don't want to find yourself in legal trouble to add to your existing problems. Try and remain as smart as possible and make all the right moves to help you repair your credit at the earliest.

Pay to delete isn't the only option available to you; you can use other strategies to repair your credit.

Check for FDCPA (Fair Debt Collection Practices Act) Violations

The law is very clear on what collection agencies can do and what they cannot do as far as debt collection is concerned. For instance:

➢ They should not call you more than once in a day unless they can prove that it was accidentally dialed by their automated systems.

➢ They cannot call you before 8.00.am or after 9.00pm.

➢ They cannot threaten, belittle or yell at you in an effort to make you pay any outstanding debts.

➢ They cannot tell anyone else other than your spouse why they are contacting you.

➢ The best way to go about this is to let them know that you are recording all their calls.

➢ They cannot take more money from your account than you have authorized if they do an ACH.

➢ They are also not allowed to send you collection letters if you have already sent them a cease and desist order.

If you can prove that collection companies are in violation of the laws, you should file a complaint with the company then have your lawyer send proof indicating the violations; you can then request that any outstanding debt be forgiven. You need to understand that the law is on your side in such circumstances; actually, if the violations are major, the collection companies could be forced to pay fines of up to $10,000 for these violations.

So, if your debt is significantly lower than this, you could be on your way to having your debt cleared since these companies would rather pay your debt than pay the fine. Every violation of the Fair Debt Collection Practices Act is punishable by a fine of up to $1000, which is payable to you so don't just think of this as something that cannot amount to anything as far as repairing your credit is concerned.

Look for Errors on your Credit Reports
Your credit report should be free of errors. Even the slightest thing as reporting the wrong date of last activity on your credit report is enough to damage your credit. As we discussed earlier on, your last date of activity has a profound effect on your credit rating. If the write off date is different from what has been reported, you can dispute the entry to have it corrected to reflect that actual status of your credit. However, keep in mind that the credit bureaus will in most instances confirm that the negative entry is correct even if this is not the case, which means that they will not remove the erroneous item.

You must put in efforts to get them on the right track. To get them to comply, you have to inform them that the law requires them to have preponderance of their systems in place to ensure that these errors do not arise. Therefore, the mere fact of confirming the initial error is not enough. Inform them about the Notice (Summons) and complaint to let them understand that you are serious about the matter. Once they have an idea of your stance, they will put in efforts to do the right thing. The thing is; the bureaus don't want any case to go to court since this could ultimately provide proof that their systems are weak or flawed, which means that they will probably be in some bigger problems.

So try and drive a strong point across so that they understand you mean business. Mere exchange of emails will not do and you must send them details on how strong your case will be. This will make them understand their position and they will decide to help you to avoid going to court. This will, in turn, work to your advantage in making them to dig deeper into the issue. However, this method will only work if you are certain that an error was actually made. You will also require proof for it and cannot simply state that there was an error.

Request proof of the original debt
If you are certain that the credit card has been written off for late payment, it is highly likely that the carriers (Capital One and Citibank) cannot find the original billing statements within 30 days, which they are required by the law to respond. This in effect allows you to have whatever entry you have disputed removed from the credit report as if it never happened.

Another handy approach is to request for the original contract that you signed to be provided to prove that you actually opened that particular credit card in the first instance. As you do this, don't just ask for "verification" since this just prompts the collection agency to "verify" that they actually received a request for collection on an account that has your name on it. Therefore, as a rule of thumb, ensure that you state clearly that you want them to provide proof of the debt including providing billing statements for the last several months and the original contract that you signed when opening the credit card account.

Pay the original creditor
When your debt is sold to collection agencies, you will probably risk having new items showing up on your credit report, which can further hurt your credit rating. However, you can stop that by sending a check with the full payment of any outstanding amount to the original creditor after which you just send a proof of payment to that collection agency and any other then request

them to delete any derogatory items they have reported from your credit report.

It is always a good idea to be in direct contact with your creditor or creditors. In fact, many of these agencies will be fully equipped to cheat you and will follow through on plans to have your report show bad credit scores. It is up to you to try and remove these "middlemen" and do the payment yourself. You could also enter into an agreement to pay a portion of the money to the creditor as full payment for the sum (the pay to delete strategy).

Under the federal law, if the original creditor accepts any payment as full payment for any outstanding debt, the collection agency has to remove whatever they have reported. This will only work if the original creditor accepts the payment; it is possible for some of the checks you pay to the original creditor to be returned to you.

Pay up your debt

The total debt owed accounts for up to 30% of your credit score so you need to put some more emphasis in ensuring that you pay up all outstanding debts. The debt that is covered in this include personal loans, credit utilization and car loan. You need to determine your credit utilization ratio (this is usually the balance that you are carrying on your revolving account versus the credit limit). The more the credit utilization is, the lower your credit score will be. In essence, you should aim at keeping your balances at no more than 30% of the credit card limit although the idea should be to aim at maintaining it at 0% since this will help you have a higher score. You could combine this strategy with the pay to delete method to help improve your credit.

It would be best for you to consider paying off your debts at the earliest. One idea is to pay more than the minimum that needs to be paid in a month. You must choose to pay at least 5% more than the minimum and try and finish paying all of your debts at the earliest. Once you are debt free, your credit scores will automatically improve. You might want to put it on a high priority list and direct a certain amount towards your loan repayment account on a monthly basis.

When you opt to pay your outstanding debts, you could use the avalanching method or the snowballing technique. In Avalanching, you pay the debts one at a time starting with the one that has the highest interest moving down to the ones with low interest rates. Just like an avalanche that starts off big and then starts losing its power towards the end.

The advantage of this method is that you get to pay off a large amount and that will take off a lot of weight from your shoulders. The amount that has the highest interest is the best to deal with first. The only disadvantage of this method is that, you will need a large sum readily available to pay off the highest value. If you are unable to come up with a large sum then you might be psychologically affected by it and not show an interest in paying off your debts on time. However, this is still the most preferred debt repayment methods and continues to be popular amongst several people.

In the snowballing method, you pay off the debts that have the lowest balance first, have them closed then move up to pay up bigger debts. Just like a snowball that starts small and then grows in size by collecting snow on its way. So look for the debts that are the lowest and list them out. Start paying them one by one. You will be happy to start repaying your debt and it will have a large impact on your psychology. You can have only a little saved up to start repaying. But the disadvantage of this method is that, the larger amounts will cause your interest to hit the roof. You will end up paying more than needed thanks to taking more time to repay them.

You must make your choice depending on how much money you have saved up. As long as you have made up your mind to repay all your outstanding debts, you must put in efforts to see it through.

Pay your bills on time

You need to understand that your payment history accounts for up to 35% of your credit score, which is one of the highest single determinants of how high or low your score will be. To ensure that you start recovering from poor credit, you should start paying your bills when they are due and it will also be good if you pay them much before their due date. Many people forget to pay on time and end up having a bad credit score. Just by paying your bills on time you will have a chance to show how good you are at paying your debts. This will instantly bring up your credit score and make you a good candidate to avail credit.

If you are having trouble remembering to pay them, then consider using an alarm as a reminder to pay on time every month. As soon as the alarm goes off you must jump into action and pay up all your bills. One of the best strategies that will ensure that you pay your bills at the agreed upon times is through setting up automatic payments that will be deducted from your account on a certain date. That is, you will link your checking or savings account to the receiver's account and they will automatically receive whatever is due to them.

You will not have to rush to pay them. With this handy technique, you will be assured that you won't forget paying important bills even when you had the money to pay. You will soon discover that your credit score will improve drastically by just paying the bills on time. This is mainly because lenders will mainly be concerned about whether you can pay your bills or not and the only way they can tell that you are a good debtor is when you have a history of paying your bills.

Such things that contribute to this 35% include bankruptcies, collections and late payments and the more recent the various delinquencies are, the more they will be factored in your credit score. Actually, up to 70% of your score is accounted by whatever has taken place in the past 2 years on your credit profile.

Start spreading/mixing credit

This accounts for just 10% of your overall credit score. Lenders prefer this because they consider you to have a good history of managing various kinds of credit, which is a plus to you if you are to apply for credit in future; this will only work if you have a positive history of paying the installments. If you need help with this then consider consulting someone with a good knowledge on the subject to help you out.

Identity theft Strategy

In a recent report, more than 16 million Americans are victims of identity theft; it could be you. If you decide to follow this route, you can be assured that whatever derogatory items are in your account will be removed if you can prove identity theft. However, this involves the police since identity theft is a crime so if you are going this direction, be ready to have the person responsible for identity theft charged for that. If you don't want to get the person responsible for stealing your identity into trouble, you should follow other methods. However, if you want to follow this route, here is how to file that issue successfully.

> ➤ If you report the matter to the police, get a copy of that report from the local sheriff since you will need this somewhere in the process.

> ➤ Use this link https://www.ftccomplaintassistant.gov/ to file a dispute with FTC.

> ➤ Move on to dispute the entry with the different credit bureaus.

After filing the dispute, set up an identity theft alert on your credit report if you want to solve many of the problems you could face in the process. For instance, no one else will access your details when you have the alert. It is best to use this service when you don't know the identity of the person who tried to access credit using your name since there will be heightened scrutiny in form of request for additional verification when applying for any credit. However, if you don't mind the inconvenience, you can go ahead with it. Don't try to be over smart and get someone to pose as a thief. If the cops find out that there is foul play then you can land in a lot of trouble. If there is genuinely a theft then don't waste too much time and deal with the person at the earliest to improve your credit score.

CAUTION

Please note that this option MUST ONLY be used when you are certain that there is identity theft. If you fail to comply, you will be committing an offense especially if no case of identity theft is found.

You can be assured that the disputed item will be deleted if fraud and identity theft is ascertained.

Handy Tips and Tricks during the Dispute Process

The credit repair process could be quite tricky if you don't know what to do. You could easily make some avoidable mistakes when you don't know what you are doing. So, how do you make sure that you don't make these mistakes? Here are some tips to help you during the dispute process.

> ➢ Never have the same dispute reason for one account. Even if you are disputing an account multiple times, ensure that each letter has a different reason to avoid instances where your dispute is marked as frivolous. This is especially true if you are disputing through E-OSCAR and OCR. It is even best to dispute multiple accounts at the same time as opposed to disputing one account multiple times, as this might make your disputes to be marked frivolous. When anything is marked frivolous, your chances of ever getting it out of your report are very slim so ensure that you don't do something that will make that happen.

➤ Send the advanced dispute letters to the creditors and not to the credit bureaus. In most instances, the creditors won't get back to you when they delete an item so check in the subsequent credit reports from your credit monitoring service.

➤ If you opt to cancel your credit cards as a strategy for improving your credit score, don't cancel the oldest line of credit first since this will make your credit history to look much younger, which will, in turn hurt your score. This is a reiteration as it is an important point to note.

➤ Never close any revolving account; instead, try to keep them forever if you can. This usually account for up to 15% of your credit score. The more time you keep them open, the more likely your credit score will be higher.

➤ Always remember to get a settlement letter once you pay your debts. Send this copy to the credit bureaus to ensure that they update your credit report immediately. Through that, your credit score should improve substantially.

- These form the best ways in which you can deal with mistakes that are present within your credit report and how you can have them rectified at the earliest. I hope you start with your proceedings at the earliest and see good results in terms of your credit scores.

Chapter 19

Other Causes For A Bad Score

So far, we have read on the mistakes that might appear on your credit report, and why these can be your credit worthiness's worst enemies, but, these wrong entries are not the only ones that will cause you to have a bad score and there will be many other reasons. Let us look at each one of these in detail.

Credit card dues

Credit cards are known as your credit report's worst enemies. It is believed that more than 3/4ths of the people in the United States rely on credit card to fund their daily buys. This means that they use their card for all sorts of purchases regardless of small or big. This will cause the person to have a lot of dues that they fail to pay on time. Ultimately, it will appear badly on their credit report as debt payments constitute 30% of the report. So it is extremely vital to settle all credit card dues at the earliest and not allow it to tamper with your credit worthiness.

Excess cards

One of the reasons why credit card dues come about is because of the presence of too many cards. Once a person buys a credit card, he or she automatically falls prey to its vicious mind controlling powers. As soon as a card maxes out, the person starts to feel anxious and to keep using the card, applies for another one. This continues until the person has 3 to 4 cards and uses all of them in a month to buy daily needs and large purchases. All of it will turn out to be extremely hefty and the person will end up with a large bill.

Maxed out cards

Maxing out on your credit cards is a wrong move. When you max out your cards, it indicates that you have used up everything that is provided to you. This will show badly on your credit score. Creditors will check if you are maxing out and prefer you. They will know you will max out theirs and probably pay late, which will help them levy fines on you. So it is important to not max out on any cards and remain within the limits on each one.

Late payments

Paying bills and other debts late will mean bad news for your credit report. Late payments reflect badly and you will have a lot of bad remarks. This will instantly bring your credit score down. If you continue with this then you might slip into the under 500 range. It is therefore important that you pay all your bills on time. If you have trouble remembering then decide to have reminders that will prompt you and make you pay on time. Some people prefer to link their checking or savings account to the creditors account and have money automatically transferred on a monthly basis.

Canceling old cards

Remember that your old credit cards are extremely important tin proving your credit worthiness. They are the cards that you bought first and contain all the important information. They will mention your timely payments and you will have a good track record. These will help your credit scores remain high. If you wish to cancel your cards then choose the ones that you had bought recently. Do not cancel any of your old cards and choose the keep the ones that have the best record. It is ideal for you to have not more than 2 cards with you.

Canceling cards with credit

Do not cancel cards that have credit. What this will do is, bring your account balance to 0$. You will still have the credit amount and yet it will show as 0$ balance. As was mentioned before, this is not a good scenario and your account balance should not go down to 0. This will impact the 30% meant for debt repayment and will cause your score to go down. So do not cancel cards that still have credit on them and try and use the credit fully before you decide to settle it and cancel the card.

Mortgage payments

Pay your mortgage on time. If in case you fail to or end up losing your house then your credit score will be impacted in the worst possible way. You must make paying mortgage a priority and not take it lightly. If your house is foreclosed then you will further lose points. If with all this you fall under the 500 or below category then you can forget about availing another housing loan as no creditor will be interested in you and even if they are then the interest rates will be unfathomable.

Hefty loans

Taking hefty loans is a bad idea. Just like mortgaging, hefty loans will cause you to have bad credit for a long time. Every month, you will have to pay excessive interest, which will be bad for your credit scores. Your credit report will appear badly and you will have problems in the future. So if you have the habit of borrowing loans often, then it is best that you improve on this habit and start repaying all your dues at the earliest. How you can pay off your debts is explained in the next chapter.

Bankruptcy

Bankruptcy is often seen as the last resort but in reality, it should not even be considered. When you file for bankruptcy, you end up brining your credit score to 0. This means that you have 0 credit worthiness and are not even worth considering. You might never have a chance to avail a loan to buy a house or a car. You must try and be done with your loans at the earliest and even if your financial situation is bad or worse must not consider filing for bankruptcy at any cost.

Remember to bear all of these points in mind if you wish your credit score to improve.

Chapter 20

Best Way To Pay Off All Debts

Remember that you need to focus on paying off all your debts at the earliest. You cannot waste any more time and must try and finish them off to have a good score. Let us now look at the things that you need to do to pay off your debts on time.

The two methods

As was mentioned earlier, you can pay off your debts in one of the two methods that are made available viz. the first one being the avalanche method and the second being the snowball method. Each type has its own advantages and disadvantages. You need to look at whatever fits your budget best and go for it without wasting any more time. If you think you have enough money saved up then choose the avalanche method but if you have very little then chose the snowballing method. Apart from these, if you have enough money to pay everything all together then you can choose that option as well.

Planning

Remember to always work with a plan. When you have everything planned out it will be easy for you to finish your task. Start by preparing a monthly budget by including your incomes and expenses and try and balance it out to remain with as much money at the end as possible. You need to add your debts to the expenses column and this will help you pay them on time. When you are left with a surplus, you can use it to open a separate "debt repayment" account and add in the money there. Once you have a substantial amount, you can use it to pay off all your debts.

Organizing

Mere planning will not suffice and you need to be as organized as possible. You must have everything in place to help you operate smoothly. Try having a different account for each of your debts so that money automatically gets transferred every month. You must also have a set monthly budget for your expenses. You must not use any more money than what you have assigned. When you are organized, you will feel that your life is easy and there are not many obstacles standing in your way.

Contact

The next step is to contact your creditors. This means that you get in touch with them and assure them that you are going to pay your debts on time. Many times, it pays to develop a good rapport with your creditors. But don't push it and remain within your limits. You need to develop a rapport and not a close friendship with them. You need to win over their trust and make them like your determination. Remain in touch with them and update them on your every move to repay their debts on time. After a while, the informality between the two of you will start to reduce.

Negotiate

When you have struck a good rapport, you can decide to ask for a small rebate in your debt or negotiate the rate of interest that you have to pay. This might not be possible with all creditors such as banks but you can try your luck with money lenders and other non commercial lenders. Once they are happy with your timely debt repayments they might decide to reduce the interest rate by a little. But don't expect them to waive off your loan as nobody will be willing to do that. You can ask them if you can pay a little less for the last few installments and count that as your rebate.

Secured credit card

When you are trying to pay off all your debts at the earliest, you must not use your credit card excessively. Your credit score will plummet and so, it is best that you give up on these. There are other alternatives to credit cards that you can consider. Debit cards are a great idea as you will only draw money from your own account when you use these. Buy if you want to have the feel of a credit card then you can opt for a secured credit card. These are issued by your bank and they will be linked to your account. You will have to add money to this account and there will be a limit on how much you can draw in a month. There will be no interest levied on the amount and you must add back the money that you withdrew within a specified period of time to help the account remain active.

Family

Sometimes, if there is a lot of debt then you can consider borrowing some money from your relatives. When you do so, you will be able to pay off a debt easily. Your family members might not charge you a high rate of interest and it might be within your budget. You can consider asking your dad or your uncle or anybody who is in a position to pay you the amount at the earliest. You need not stress over paying the sum back to them and can do it leisurely and at your own pace.

Life insurance

It is also possible for you to borrow money from your life insurance policy. You can ask for a certain amount that you promise to pay back within a specified period of time. Once approved, you can use the money to pay off your debts or at least a majority of it. There is no interest as such that will be levied on this sum and you can repay it after a few years' time. Once you repay your debt and give back to your insurance company then you will truly be free and your credit score will start to rise high.

Bank borrowing

It pays to have everything unified to make for easy payments. This means that you can borrow a certain amount from your bank and pay off all your creditors in bulk. You can then pay only to your bank to settle your debts. This will make it easier for you as you have to pay to only one institution. The rate of interest might also be low and that will help you save on a lot of money. The only disadvantage of this type is that, not many banks entertain this sort of borrowing. But you can try your luck and approach two or more banks with a proposal.

Money savers

Every month, think of ways in which you can save on money. This can be by way of using coupons while shopping or making use of store credit to help save on the bill etc. You can also sell your old and unused stuff to make some money out of it. It is also a good idea to gift a service instead of a physical gift as this will further help you in saving money. But if you cannot gift a service every time then you can consider buying them in bulk after the holiday is over and store it to be gifted the next year. Cutting down on electricity, water and gas bills will also help you save money. It is also ideal for you to buy second hand goods for the time being and save further.

You can follow these steps to repay all your loans at the earliest and improve your credit score.

Chapter 21

Last Resort

By now, you have read about the credit system, credit scores, the importance of raising your scores, disputing erroneous entries, other reasons for a bad score and how you can fix these. All these processes can take a lot of your time and effort and not everybody has this much time to spend on fixing their credit. For this purpose, it is better to enlist the help of a "credit repair company" that will do the job for you by charging you pay a small fee for it.

Let us look at this topic in detail.

Credit repair companies

Credit repair companies are those that help you in foxing your bad credit scores. Approaching these companies is seen as the last resort as most people will try and fix their bad credit themselves but if they are incapable then they will turn to seek help. The main job of these companies is to help people fix their bad scores and so, they will have an expertise in the field. They will have people dedicated to looking for the errors, expert opinions, forwarding the advice etc. So once you decide to avail their help, you can remain relaxed.

The process that these companies follow is simple. They will ask for a copy of your credit report (they will only take the ones that have been procured from the three leading credit agencies viz. TransUnion, Experian and Equifax) and go through it thoroughly. Once they are done, they will look for erroneous entries that you can dispute. These entries need to be disputed at the earliest and for this they will revert back as soon as possible. Once you receive their response, you can go ahead with the disputing process. They will also contact the credit agencies to challenge the items on your credit report that does not appear to be right.

People prefer to trust these companies when they are not able to find the mistakes themselves or don't have the time and patience to dispute it. These companies will help them expedite the process and get done with it at the earliest. Although they will not have the power to do something that is above and beyond your own capacity, they will help it make a smoother and easier process. They will go about it in the same way as you would except that you have now outsourced the job to these companies.

Looking for the best

When it comes to trusting a third party with your personal information, it will be obvious that you will have a few reservations against it. This is only natural as nobody will be interested in divulging their personal information to others. But if you find the right company that is not interested in anything except helping you fix your credit then you can share your details without worry. But for this, you need to look for the best company.

Here are some guidelines for you to choose the right company for yourself.

 ➢ You must not trust a company that is charging you money even before looking at your credit report. No company is supposed to take your money until they have done the job for you.

 ➢ You must not trust companies that are not explaining you're your rights in detail or telling you what you can and cannot do while you dispute your score.

 ➢ You cannot trust a company that is asking you to not contact the credit agencies by yourself and that they will do it for you.

> ➤ If your credit company is telling you to take some illegal action then it is best that you not pursue the case further.

These are some of the standard criteria that you must consider when you look for a credit repair company.

Rates and other information

It is important that you consider the rates that are charged by these companies. If the company is over charging for the service that they are providing then you need not consider them. You need to find out from others how much they are paying for a credit repair service and pay similar fees. You need to look at the brochure that mentions all the services that they will provide and also a fee break up if it is available. Check if they are providing you with any guarantees. Most companies do not guarantee anything as it will be a risk for them. But if the company is experienced enough and has a lot of confidence in solving any kind of problem then they might give you a few guarantees.

You must also look at the time that they have specified to deliver their service. It should be not any more than 1 or 2 weeks and the earlier the better. If they are giving you a detailed analysis then you can wait for a couple of weeks and not any more. Finally, make sure that you have all their contact details. You must have access to their address and phone numbers. You must be able to visit them and call them at any time. Once you get your report and have decided to dispute the entries, you can pay the company whatever is due to them.

Key highlights

The very first thing to be aware of is the importance of credit. Credit is an extremely important part of life. You might not have enough money to buy yourself a house or a car and will need help in raising enough money for these. This money can be borrowed from financial institutions or credit companies and the borrowed sum is known as "credit". But you need to have a decent credit score if you wish to avail this credit. Once your credit is approved, you can make the purchases but will have to repay the borrowed money along with an interest amount.

The next step is to understand the credit system. The credit system can be good or bad and depends on how you interpret it. Generally, the credit companies consult the credit bureaus to find them people with a bad score. What this does is, helps them in charging these people with a higher rate of interest. And so, the two will join hands to trap customers that have a low credit score and try and pull as much money from them as possible. But if you have a good score then you will avail a credit at the lowest possible rate from any of these credit companies.

A good credit score is vital for everybody. You need to work on fixing your credit scores and getting into a higher category. The higher you are placed, the better your chances of availing a loan at low rates of interest. You, and your family members, will need money to conduct your day to day activities and if you have a bad score then you will not be able to avail credit. So it is important that you try and fix your credit score at the earliest and not waste too much time.

You must approach the credit agency to avail a free copy of your credit report. Once you have it, you need to go through it in detail to find any mistakes in it. If there are mistakes then you must make a note of them. Some of these can be a mistake in the date of your last transaction, errors in your personal information, erroneous entries, two creditors mentioning the same entry etc. Once you have figured out all the mistakes, you need to move to the next step in the process of fixing your bad credit score.

To fix these errors, you need to approach the credit company that has made the mistake. If they agree to help you, which they probably never will, then well and good but if they don't, then you need to take measures to comply. You can choose to pay them to fix the errors and delete the erroneous entries or threaten to take them to court. You can also register a complaint with the cops in case you are a victim of identity threat. As long as you successfully get your mistakes rectified it will be all good but if it is not working for you, then you can consider the last resort.
Apart from wrong entries that are made by the credit companies or the credit bureaus, other reasons can also cause you to have bad credit. These can include not paying your debts on time, having a lot of credit card dues, not paying your mortgage on time, defaulting on borrowings, filing for bankruptcy etc. All of these will ultimately affect your credit score the wrong way. You might slip into the bad or poor category, which will spell doom for your credit availing chances.

It is best that you fix these issues at the earliest. You will have to make up your mind to pay off all your debts as soon as possible and not have them loom over your head. You must also have a plan to repay your mortgage and try and be done within a year or two. You must put in efforts to save money and invest it to have enough for your future. You can also direct a part of this towards repaying any of your old loans. The two methods to repay being avalanche and snowballing and you can choose the one that suits you the best.

Whatever the situation, it is never a good idea to file for bankruptcy. You might be tempted to file for it to avail instant freedom from all your troubles but remember that you will probably lose all your chances of availing credit in the future. You need to consider the ill effects first before you proceed. But once you do file for it, you will probably be left with very few personal assets and have a tough time leading a normal life. So it is wise to not file for bankruptcy and remain positive. You can always consider the last resort of consulting a professional credit repair agency to help you out.

Credit repair agencies are neither good nor bad. They will mostly be neutral as it is their job to try and help you repair your credit. There are not many things in this world that come with a guarantee and credit repair companies are one such option. If you are feeling overwhelmed by your low credit score and in no position to fix the problem yourself then don't think twice before enlisting the help of a credit repair company.

Glossary

Credit

Credit is the money that you borrow from a company to pay for your expenses. You might not have enough money to pay for everything that you need on a monthly basis and might have to borrow it from someone. They will lend you the money to be used for your purchases but you must repay it to them within a specified period of time.

Interest rates

When someone lends you money, he or she will not lend it without charging an interest for it. The interest is a fixed percentage that they will charge and you must pay the sum that is above and beyond what you borrowed. They will have to make a profit out of lending money to others and this they do by levying an interest on the sum. This interest differs from person to person depending on their credit worthiness.

Credit report

Credit report is a statement that is prepared for an individual or a firm and includes all their financial transactions and determines their credit worthiness. The statement will clearly mention the person's borrowing, his or her payment history, dues, fines etc. The report is used to check whether the person is worth giving credit to or not. Banks and credit agencies will prepare these. These reports are free of cost and can be availed from a national credit agency.

Credit scores

Credit scores are awarded to a person depending on their credit worthiness. This means that they will fall under a specific credit category which will determine their worthiness. Here are the scores.

300-580: Poor
581-650: Bad
651-710: Average
711-750: Good
751 and up: Excellent

Depending on what score the person has, he or she will be judged for their credit worthiness.

Creditworthiness

Credit worthiness refers to understanding how well a person can be entrusted with a loan or money. It is used to determine how much money can be given away in the form of a loan. If the person has a score that is above 720 or 750 then the person is extremely credit worthy but if it is below 500 then the person is not at all credit worthy.

Credit limit

Credit limit is the amount that a person is allowed to borrow from a company or a card. The limit is fixed based on the person's ability to repay a loan. The limit is mainly placed for the person to remain within the confines of whatever he or she is capable of paying. But if the person exceeds the limit then that can be a bad thing.

Credit companies

Credit companies are those that give away credit to a person. They can be individuals or firms such as money lenders and banks and will issue credit to whoever approaches them, given that they are credit worthy. They will check the person's credit report and scores and then determine if they are worth issuing credit.

Credit bureaus

Credit bureaus keep a track of your transactions. They will collect all your information and supply it to credit companies. They will charge a small fee for this service from the companies but given the number of companies that they cater to, they will easily make a large profit.

National credit agencies

National credit agencies are those that prepare a person's credit report. These agencies can be directly contacted to avail a free copy of the report. They will take not more than 15 days to prepare and send a copy to the person. The main national credit agencies include Equifax, TransUnion and Experian. Any or all of these can be contacted for the copy.

Credit repair

Credit repair refers to fixing a bad credit score. There can be many reasons for a bad score to come about but one of the main reasons is said to be erroneous entries made by spurious creditors and credit companies. These entries will cause the person to have a bad score but there can be other reasons for it as well.

Erroneous entries

Erroneous entries are those wrong and incorrect entries that are made by indecent creditors and credit bureaus and might include wrong dates, wrong personal information, duplication of entries etc. all of these will impact the person's credit scores in a negative way. These need to be checked and dealt with.

Disputing

Disputing refers to moving the creditors to fix the mistakes that are committed in your credit report. You must get them to comply and make them clean your credit report to improve your scores.

Defaulting

Defaulting refers to not paying the borrowed amount in full. The person will not pay the full sum to the creditor and will not be able to do so owing to insufficient funds. Defaulting has a negative impact on the person's credit score.

Fico score

The fico score is a credit risk score that was introduced by the Fair Isaac Corporation. It is a mathematical system them helps you calculate your exact score and allows you to check your credit worthiness. You must make use of this to check if what the credit bureau has supplied you with is correct.

Bankruptcy

Bankruptcy refers to claiming having no money left to repay any of the debts. When a person files for bankruptcy their credit balance will come down to 0. This will be extremely bad for their credit score which will also be 0. They will find it hard to avail credit further in their life. There are two ways in which a person can deal with their debts. Either trust a third party to sell their assets and repay the debts or hold on to them and sell them themselves to pay the debts in full.

Conclusion

Thank you again for purchasing this book and hope you had a good read!

I hope this book was able to help learn how to repair your credit.

More often than not, using credit cards both for small and big purchases causes trouble for most people. The most common reason is missing out on payments in a timely manner, which may be due to oversight, financial emergencies or tight financial state.

While credit repair may be a simple process, it could take most of your time as well as effort. As you have learned from this book, you need to obtain a copy of your credit report. Remember, you have the right to request for your credit history from the concerned credit bureau or reporting agency. You can also download your credit report from the agency's website for a certain fee.

There are three credit reporting agencies from which you can obtain your credit report. These are the Equifax, Experian, and Transunion. You can also check out their websites and download your credit report from each of them.

Once you have a copy of your credit history, examine it thoroughly. It is best if you compare each item with your stubs of payments and spending. For any inaccuracy, mistake, or discrepancy, make sure to contact the concerned credit bureau and request for an investigation on the item in question. Make sure to request the investigation once you have found out about the inaccuracy so that you can take action immediately and proceed to repairing your credit. It is also advisable to establish a timeline once you have requested for an investigation from the credit bureau. Check with the agency again if they fail to respond within your timeline or within 30 days. In the event that the credit agency does not respond within 30 days, request for the removal of the item in question from your credit report. Again, it is your right to have it removed due to noncompliance of the agency.

On the other hand, if there is no inaccuracy in your report and you admit that your bad credit situation is your own doing, you should monitor your finances in a serious way. Make sure to plan your finances. For instance, cut down on unnecessary spendings and/ or pay your creditor the full amount due. Most creditors provide their customers with an additional time to pay up debts; however, it would only add up to your expenses if you delay your payment.

When you are dealing with a creditor, it is best to let them know that you are serious about repairing your credit. More often than not, creditors appreciate the effort of their customers in repaying their debts as it saves both time and effort. However, make sure that whatever deal you come up with, you would stick to your word.

The process of credit repair may be a daunting and time-consuming task. However, it is also a circumstance from which you can learn. For instance, you would learn to use your credit wisely once you obtain a good credit rating given that you would not want to go through the entire credit repair process again. You learn how to manage your finances and budget more efficiently than before. You also learn to control your spending urges, specifically those transpiring at the spur of the moment. Finally, you learn how important it is to keep copies of your credit card and payment stubs. Keeping a copy of your stubs could be useful in the future, should you find any discrepancy in your credit report.

The main aim of this book was to educate you on the topic of credit repair and what you must do to fix yours. Regardless of whether you have a low score or a medium one, it is possible for you to fix it just by taking a few right steps in the right direction.

The next step is to request your credit report from the credit bureaus or subscribe to a credit monitoring service, which will be sending you monthly credit reports from all the three main credit bureaus.

Once you have done that, the next step is to go through each credit report ensuring to check or ascertain the accuracy of all entries to ensure that they are correctly stated.

If anything is not stated, as it should, find which strategy we have discussed here could work best for your situation then follow that method to dispute any derogatory items from your credit report. As you do that, don't give up easily; the credit bureaus pry on people like you who give up on their right. Even as you continue disputing derogatory items from your credit report, you need to study the relevant laws to ensure that you can use the law to your benefit to even get more derogatory items removed from your credit report.

Once your credit is repaired, you will feel happy and have a chance to buy a house, a car, secure your future etc. You will also be able to make your family members happy and they will lead a merry life.

If you received value from this book, then I'd like to ask you for a small favor. Would you be kind enough to leave a review for this book on Amazon?

I want to reach as many people as I can with this book, and the more reviews will help me accomplish that!

Not only that you will get some good karma as well.

Thank you for your time. I wish you the best of luck.

Richard

Check Out My Other Books

Below you'll find some of my other books that are popular on Amazon and Kindle as well.

Debt-Free: How to Get Out Of Debt to Your Road towards Financial Freedom

Personal Finance: 7 Steps To Effective Budgeting and Money Management To Build Personal Wealth